M*A*S*H

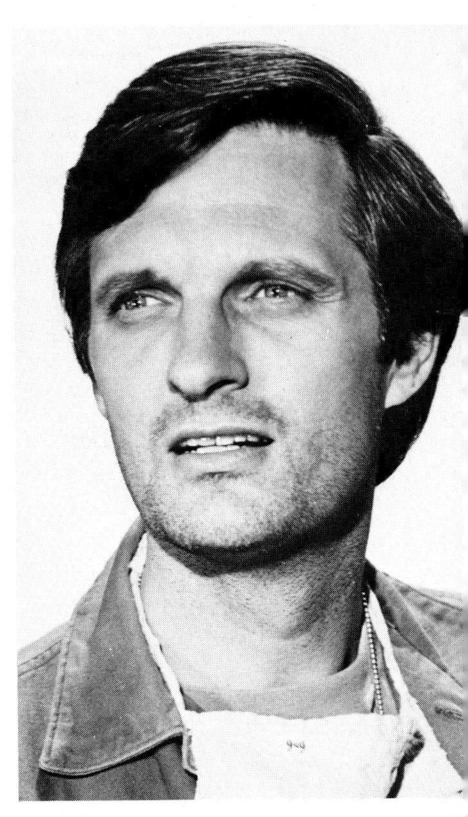

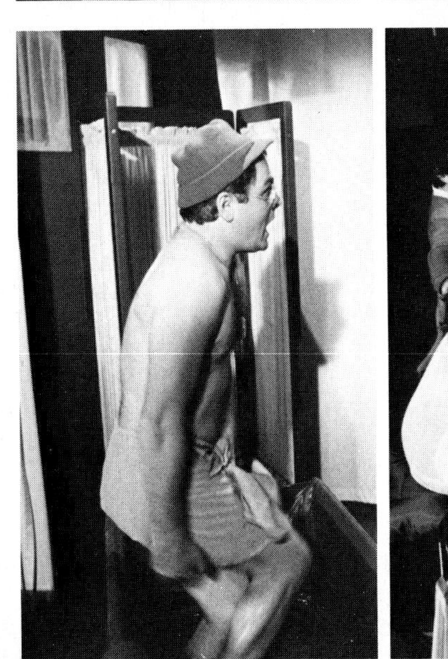

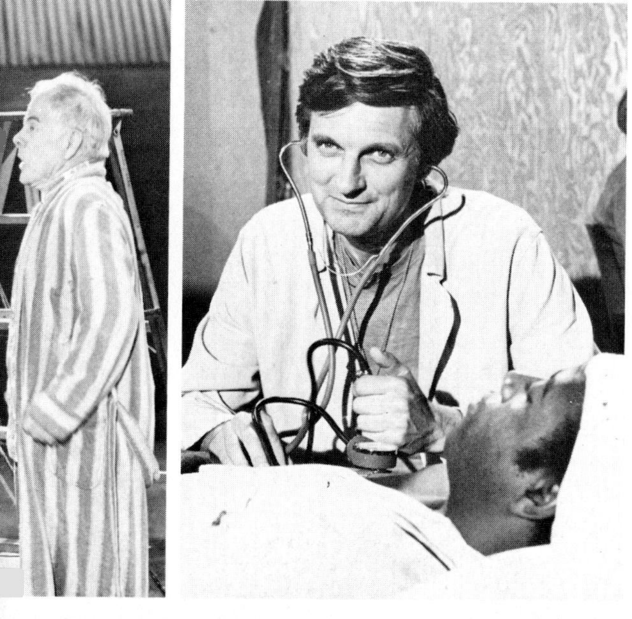

M*A*S*H

The Exclusive, Inside Story of TV's Most Popular Show

David S. Reiss

Foreword by Alan Alda

The Bobbs-Merrill Company, Inc.
Indianapolis/New York

Published by The Bobbs-Merrill Company, Inc.
Indianapolis New York

Cover and interior design by Marcia Ben-Eli

Library of Congress Cataloging in Publication Data

Reiss, David S.
M*A*S*H: the exclusive inside story of TV's most popular show.

1. Mash (Television program) I. Title: Mash.
PN1992.77.M2843R44 791.45'72 80-685
ISBN 0-672-52656-5 (pbk.)

Contents

Acknowledgments

*I would like first to acknowledge the assistance of Twentieth Century–Fox and the entire cast, crew, and production staff of M*A*S*H, without whose help this book could never have been written.*

I would like to thank the most wonderful research assistant/sounding board any writer could ever hope to find—Joyce Thompson. Also to my typist, punctuator, and dictionary, Jill Colucci, my eternal gratitude. These two hard-working women stuck by me throughout this project. I could not have done it without them.

I would also like to acknowledge the gentle prodding, wonderful suggestions, and constant support of Frank and Karen Lieberman, two genuine friends.

Finally, I would like to acknowledge the aid and support of Alan Alda, whose respect and concern for quality have helped to preserve the intent of this book.

*All M*A*S*H photographs by Twentieth Century–Fox and David S. Reiss.*

This book is dedicated to the following very special people with more love than mere words can express:

To my parents, for being the two most unselfish, giving human beings, who have stood by me with love and support through everything. To you, I owe it all.

To my sister Carol, for growing up with me.

To Gail Dubov, whose friendship I will share until eternity.

To Charles S. Dubin, brilliant director, teacher, giving human being, and a man whom I am proud to call my friend.

To Mike and Judy Farrell, two of the most genuine people I have ever encountered. It has been my fortune to share their love and warmth.

SEOUL 34 MI 54 Km
SAN FRANCISCO

Foreword

It's been a little like being in a real M*A*S*H unit.

There's been the sleeplessness and fatigue—the lack of time, of facilities—too much heat and too much cold. And, at times, even bad food and not enough time to eat it.

But there's also been the pulling together and the growth of loyalties and friendships and a sense of pride in what we were doing. We felt we were involved in something bigger than ourselves, and it kept us going.

We were nourished and sustained by the feeling that we were doing something of value.

Just as the original M*A*S*H people had first been put there to keep the Army machine going and then found themselves caught up in the saving of lives, we had been assembled to keep the television machinery humming along and later found out that if we tried hard enough and cared enough we could do more than just fill time—we could explore compassion and we could rage against death and pain. In the beginning, not everyone knew what our show could become. We came in to tell jokes and stayed to touch the edges of art.

The crucial ingredients, I think, were the caring and the trying.

From my first week at the studio, when Gene Reynolds and I wheedled and cajoled the executives to keep to a shooting schedule that included a day's rehearsal for every show, we knew we were trying for quality. Rehearsal is expensive, but it gives the actors and the writers a chance to find things that are new, instead of throwing together a bunch of gags that have worked before. Originality is unexplored territory. You get there by carrying a canoe—you can't take a taxi.

But no matter how you wheedle, time and money are still limited. And caring is accomplished mainly by getting less sleep.

We threw ourselves into M*A*S*H and we let it soak up our nights and days.

I remember going with Larry Gelbart to a Chinese restaurant one night after a twelve- or fifteen-hour day to talk about story ideas; and then, after climbing wearily into our cars, still unable to let go, we stopped at every red light on Wilshire Boulevard and called ideas to each other through our open car windows.

Larry frequently stayed up all night in order to have a finished script for us on rehearsal day, and sometimes so did I. We were infected somehow by the characters we had created and were living their lives. I remember many mornings standing in the shower with my face turned to the spray trying to unglue my eyelids. And you never forget that special ache at night when you lie down and can hear your bones moaning to one another. But these years still are the best time we've ever spent—and I don't think any of us feels we'll ever know anything like it again. The working conditions may have been rough—the lack of air every time we'd shoot a scene in The Swamp, the icy drafts that blew through the holes in the roof of Stage 9, even the occasional infestation of fleas in the bed ticking—but we learned to keep pushing on, and that will keep us going all our lives.

When we look back on this, I think we'll be grateful for having learned how far caring can take you. And for having had the luck to be among this many people who cared this much. We'll be glad we had this unique concept that is M*A*S*H, and we'll be glad we had one another.

I won't forget the laughing jags that went on for fifteen minutes at a time, or the gripe sessions that seemed to go on forever but always brought us closer.

Or the pizza and beer on Friday nights.

Or the way the crew and actors ribbed one another and helped us all get through the day.

I won't forget the dozens of people who have been M*A*S*H over the years

—The genial brilliance of Larry Gelbart;
—The meticulous decency of Gene Reynolds;
—The gentle, bearded wisdom of Burt Metcalfe;
—The ring of Wayne Rogers' laugh and the encouragement of his smile;
—The artful nutsyness of McLean Stevenson;
—Both the utter seriousness and the maniacal giggle of Larry Linville;
—The intelligence of Mike Farrell and the bearhug of his friendship;
—The impish playfulness and granite dependability of Harry Morgan;
—The pluck and warmth and strength of Loretta Swit;
—The gallant striving for excellence of David Ogden Stiers;
—The talent and skill of Gary Burghoff;
—The heart and joy of Jamie Farr;
—And the sweet goodness of Bill Christopher.

These people will never leave my head. I'm very glad I have had the pleasure of their company.

—Alan Alda
May 1980

In The Beginning

The History of M*A*S*H

M*A*S*H is a unique experience for many people. For Dr. Richard Hornberger (author of the original M*A*S*H novel under the pseudonym Richard Hooker), it was his life for a year and a half during the Korean War. Hornberger was a surgeon of a M*A*S*H unit where he worked twelve-hour shifts attempting to put the wounded back into one piece.

Twelve years later, excited by the prospect of recording his experience as a surgeon in the Korean War, Dr. Hornberger set out to write the novel M*A*S*H. Upon its completion, the only task remaining was to sell it to a publisher. It was not simple. Hornberger explains, "I had 17 rejections, which was an all-time record for the agency that represented me. Various publishing companies said the female audience would reject the book because it was too dirty, or some nonsense like that. They gave a variety of excuses that those people have for something they don't want to buy or sell."

The novel M*A*S*H went on to become a best-seller and caught the attention of filmmaker Robert Altman, who, with a screenplay by Ring Lardner, Jr., created for Twentieth Century–Fox the motion picture M*A*S*H, starring Elliot Gould, Donald Sutherland, and Sally Kellerman.

The phenomenal success of the film led to Fox's decision to create a pilot for television and eventually a series which they offered to producer/director Gene Reynolds. Gene, with the assistance of writer Larry Gelbart and casting director/associate producer Burt Metcalfe, took the essence of M*A*S*H and created a part of television history.

This book is about the M*A*S*H experience. To those who have participated it is very special—as special as the M*A*S*H television series has been to a large portion of the world population.

The M*A*S*H experience is largely visceral and should really float in through one's pores and soak into one's senses. The enormous energy that abounds within the people involved is something to

Far left: Rehearsing a scene in the compound (left to right: script supervisor Roberta Scellza, guest star Pat Hingle, director Charles S. Dubin, Loretta Swit, David Ogden Stiers, Alan Alda, Harry Morgan and dialogue coach Marty Lowenheim). Left: Medical advisor for the series Walter D. Dishell, M.D., assists Loretta, Gary, Mike, and Alan in a surgical procedure. Center: Director Charles S. Dubin lines up a shot through the camera.

be seen, felt, and touched in any way possible.

A visit to the M*A*S*H set is a fascinating journey into one of the most interesting working situations in television. Stage 9 at Twentieth Century–Fox Studios (where M*A*S*H is filmed) is an old stage and much smaller than most other stages at the studio. You enter this stage only to have many illusions shattered and, magically, many new ones formed.

Your first view is the officers' club, with its roof 15 feet higher than the walls (of which there are only three), and assorted lighting instruments mounted on all sides. You look up to see that the ceiling of Stage 9 is a labyrinth of catwalks, cables and lights. Walking deeper into the stage, you come upon the mess tent and the operating room. As with the officers' club, these sets also have only three walls and lighting equipment mounted everywhere. There is little you might recognize of those sets that have become so well known on your television screen. Turn the corner and you have entered the M*A*S*H compound. Barely 90 feet long and 45 feet wide, the compound is smaller than expected, with the majestic Korean landscape painted on a backdrop that encompasses barely a third of the stage. The floor, composed of a rubber compound, is dotted by bushes, rocks, and assorted piles of dirt for authenticity. The tents have little inside them, as each set is decorated as the need arises.

The first day of each show is set aside for rehearsal. Attired in street clothes and quite at ease, the actors, writers, producers, director, and technical crew sit at a long table and begin the process of dissecting the script. The set is open only to those directly involved in the rehearsal process, thus protecting the privacy and emotional vulnerability encountered, much as a family's life becomes totally private when all visitors are gone.

After the first read-through, everyone goes through the script one page at a time and all are encouraged to offer feed-back. If an actor who knows and wishes to protect his or her character objects to a line of dialogue, the question is openly discussed, and, more times than not, the line is altered or omitted to help improve the quality of the story and to keep the character true to its nature.

Executive producer Burt Metcalfe (the only original remaining producer after Gene Reynolds' and Larry Gelbart's departure) leads the group through the various discussions and readings until 12:30 P.M.; at that point the actors and writers break for lunch until two. From 12:30 to 1:30, the members of the technical crew sit with Burt and the director to discuss technical considerations for the show and the props and special equipment required.

After lunch the director spends the afternoon running through the show with the actors and cameraman. During this process the free exchange of creative expression continues as the director and cast are encouraged to experiment and offer suggestions to further embellish the material. Despite the loose atmosphere and a great deal of horsing around, this is one of the most serious and intense work situations. All interpretations and bits of action created here will carry over to the final show that you eventually see.

The next day's shooting begins and you enter the stage to a rumbling of voices. The actors are milling about as technical crews adjust equipment, set decorators add the finishing touches, and the director looks over his script before the shooting begins. The energy and excitement are electrifying.

Looking at the cast sitting in the officers' club, you see Alan Alda reading his mail while Loretta Swit, sewing needlepoint, engages Henry Morgan in conversation. Mike Farrell plays Scrabble with Jamie Farr, Bill Christopher plays ragtime music on the piano, and David Stiers listens to classical music on headphones. Finally, a horn sounds twice, signaling that all is ready to begin.

David Stiers, still with headphones on ears and recorder on belt, slides onto his skateboard and rolls onto the set, followed by Alan Alda on his bicycle, Mike Farrell on his unicycle, and everyone else skipping along, while Harry Morgan falls behind in a gallant attempt to trip Jamie Farr.

All take their places. The bell rings and there is silence. Voices call, "Roll camera! Speed! Mark!" and the director calls, "Action!" This talented ensemble shine for the camera as they shoot a touching, sentimental scene. The director yells, "Cut!" and the first thing you notice is Jamie Farr falling on a cot as Harry Morgan has succeeded in tripping him.

The next day's shooting is at Malibu Creek State Park located in the Santa Monica mountains where the original set of the M*A*S*H compound still remains from the feature film. It is here that all outdoor scenes are shot, to be spliced later with the scenes from Stage 9. As the outdoor set is used during the summer months, the cast and crew have become accustomed to heat that often soars beyond 100 degrees. It will be a long day of shooting with dust blown into everyone's face from the helicopter.

Back at the studio and across the lot from Stage 9 is the Old Writer's Building (originally built as a school for Fox's child stars), where the producers and writing staff sit around a table working on scripts for upcoming shows and rewrites of current shows.

As M*A*S*H begins its ninth season, executive producer Burt Metcalfe leads producer John Rappaport, executive script consultants Thad Mumford and Dan Wilcox, and executive story editor Dennis Koenig toward a goal of 25 stories. They begin their work in March (shooting begins in July and ends in January) and finish the final post-production in February of the following year. To watch these men work is to see total concentration focused on the design and development of a story.

The M*A*S*H experience, for me, is the confirmation that intelligence, good taste, and a driving desire for quality do not have to be achieved at the expense of sensitivity, compassion, love, and the dignity of other human beings.

I visited the M*A*S*H set one day as a guest; I stayed two years. After saying repeatedly, "I've spent so much time on M*A*S*H, I could write a book," I did.

The Players

Alan Alda

Wickedly witty, quick with a quip or a comeback, Hawkeye Pierce is a dedicated, talented surgeon, court jester, passionate advocate of justice, instigator of endless mischief, and puncturer of pomposity. In the midst of a terrible war, he is forced, complaining and irritated, flailing away with words and gestures, to change and grow and learn something about his own very human nature.

Alan Alda is the star of the television series M*A*S*H. The character he plays, chief surgeon Benjamin Franklin "Hawkeye" Pierce, is, by his nature, personality, and life-force, the star of the M*A*S*H 4077th Unit in Korea. Part D'Artagnan, part Peter Pan, Pierce also exhibits a wide streak of Don Juan.

Larry Gelbart, writer of the original M*A*S*H pilot and one of the guiding spirits for the series' first four years, says about Alan Alda, "He's the link-pin. The cast can change, but the starting pitcher is always there. Alan Alda has come to represent M*A*S*H."

The newspaperman and writer Don Freeman has eloquently expressed the way in which Alda generates a kind of force that is central to the entire show. "I think if I have a favorite television show, it would have to be M*A*S*H, a series whose generating force, the wellspring of its shifting moods, is an actor named Alan Alda."

Attempting to describe the phenomenon that is Alan Alda, Freeman adds, "Alda, through some curious and mysterious alchemy, can register emotions that cut through the marrow of human experience. It is his gift, a peculiar genius that goes beyond the demands of craft, to transport an audience as he articulates utter despair and compassion and monstrous fatigue and the wildest, most rarified kind of humanity—all with surpassing honesty, which is also the hallmark of the show itself."

Meeting Alan Alda for the first time is a shock to

someone familiar only with the world-weary, rapid-fire, quicksilver quality of his M*A*S*H creation Hawkeye Pierce. He's taller than one might expect (6 feet, 2½ inches), quieter, and more courteous than Hawkeye. He's as warm as expected—but the careful, measured, orderly way in which he gathers his thoughts and answers questions is a surprising delight.

The son of actor Robert Alda, a theater and film star for many years, Alan Alda continues a distinguished theater tradition. He was born in New York City on January 28 (as Alphonso D'Abruzzo), and began his theatrical career at the age of 16 in summer stock in Barnesville, Pennsylvania. He attended Fordham University (during his junior year, he studied in Paris and went to Rome to perform on stage and television with his father). After his graduation from Fordham, he acted at the Cleveland Playhouse on a Ford Foundation grant. He received valuable training with the popular improvisational revues "Second City" in New York City and "Compass" in Hyannisport, Massachusetts, which served as perfect preparation for his work as a regular on the popular, satirical television show of the 60s, "That Was the Week That Was."

Alan made his breakthrough on Broadway in the tour de force, two-person comedy *The Owl and the Pussycat* costarring with Diana Sands, for which he earned critical raves. He appeared in *Purlie Victorious; Fair Game For Love,* winning a Theatre World Award; and was "Adam" to Barbara Harris's "Eve" in the musical *The Apple Tree,* for which he received a Tony nomination.

Alan made his feature film debut in *Gone Are The Days,* the movie version of his stage success *Purlie Victorious.* In preparation for his film roles, he has often immersed himself in extensive research, exploring Kentucky outlaw-whiskey country for *The Moonshine Wars,* studying piano technique for *The Mephisto Waltz,* and learning the basics of football in order to play journalist George Plimpton in *Paper Lion.*

On television he appeared in, among others, "The Glass House" and the 90-minute special of the Broadway hit "6 Rms Riv Vu" with Carol Burnett. He also received an Emmy nomination for his portrayal of Caryl Ghessman in "Kill Me If You Can."

Alan is one of the few television stars whose talent and popularity allow him to move freely and successfully between television and feature films. He did three major films in the six-month hiatus between the seventh and eighth seasons of M*A*S*H: *Same Time Next Year*, *California Suite*, and *The Seduction of Joe Tynan*, having written the last one of these as well.

The part of Hawkeye Pierce was among the two or three key roles to be cast before the pilot for the proposed M*A*S*H TV series could go into rehearsal. Alan Alda was Gene Reynolds' and Larry Gelbart's first and only choice for this vital role, but their final deadline was upon them before they received an answer from him. Alda was in Utah at the state prison shooting "The Glass House" when Larry Gelbart's script for the pilot was sent to him. "It was the best pilot script I had ever read," Alan recalls. "I was very interested in talking to them about it, but I wanted to make sure that the war was *not* going to be taken lightly."

He finished filming at the prison only a day or so before the pilot rehearsals were to begin and he still had not agreed to accept the part. At a meeting with Reynolds and Gelbart, they assured him that they shared his concerns about the series—that the show would not express a "madcap-men-at-war, fun-and-games-in-the-army" kind of concept. Alan was impressed with what Reynolds and Gelbart had to say. An agreement was reached at 2:00 A.M., and a few hours later, at 10:00 A.M., rehearsal began.

Alan resists wherever possible talking too analytically about the Hawkeye character. He feels he has to live with the character, and stepping away from it too much, getting too intellectual about it, limits the possibilities of the character's development. When he writes a segment for M*A*S*H he finds he can write the characterization for Hawkeye, but trying to talk about Hawkeye in a way that would pigeonhole him doesn't come easily to Alan. When pressed, he says, "In some ways we're alike, in that we both care a lot about our work and we're dedicated to it. We both care about people and we get offended at injustice. On the other hand, I don't drink the way he does. I don't chase women the way he does. And I'm not interested in the sight of blood—but it doesn't seem to bother *him*."

Asked what characteristics of Hawkeye he is particularly fond of, some of his reluctance to discuss the role melts in the delight he obviously feels for his alter ego: "I really like his passion. I like his appetite. He throws himself into what he does. I like his dedication to his work, his responsibility, and I like his ability to cut through his own seriousness with a self-deprecating joke." Alda recalls an incident in which Hawkeye was making a speech about how much everybody in the camp meant to him and he looked at Trapper, played by Wayne Rogers, and asked, "How am I doing on the humility meter?" "He cuts through his own pomposity," Alda notes.

Alan goes on to talk more generally about Hawkeye. "The show has been running for eight seasons, and although Hawkeye is the same person he was at

An early photograph of Alan, from his parents' photo album.

the beginning of the series, more complexities have been revealed. The darker side of Hawkeye has been shown—his pettiness now and again, and his occasional jealousy of the people around him. One doesn't dislike him, because his essential decency has been shown again and again, but, like everybody else, he's given to human frailty."

It's a special delight for Alan to be able to show this very human side of an otherwise heroic figure, and most of the episodes he writes gently point out a flaw or two in Hawkeye.

Alan, Gary, and Mike in a scene from "Welcome to Korea."

A key ingredient of Hawkeye's character and one that makes him so attractive to millions of fans is his refusal to knuckle under to authority. He accepts an order only if it seems reasonable and not because *any* authority carries any weight with him whatsoever, and Hawkeye *never* salutes. He gives officers a little wave or returns a salute with a waggle of his fingers. The only people he has ever saluted are people for whom he feels affection. He saluted Radar (Gary Burghoff) when Radar left for home, and Father Mulcahy (Bill Christopher) when the priest received his captain's bars. That's been *it* for Hawkeye's saluting over the eight years of M*A*S*H.

The one aspect of Hawkeye that Alan *can't* understand, and a major difference between them, is Pierce's resistance to marriage. Alan says: "He seems to be actively resisting getting married, and that interests me. I don't know why he's like that. The two or three times he's been tempted to think about sharing his life with somebody, it's come over him like a bad cold, and he shakes it off after a while." Alan Alda has been married to his wife Arlene since he was 21 and admits to being more in love with her every day. Alan feels his marriage and his family are of paramount importance in his life.

Alan met Arlene at an evening of chamber music

Alan *à la* "Groucho" Alda.

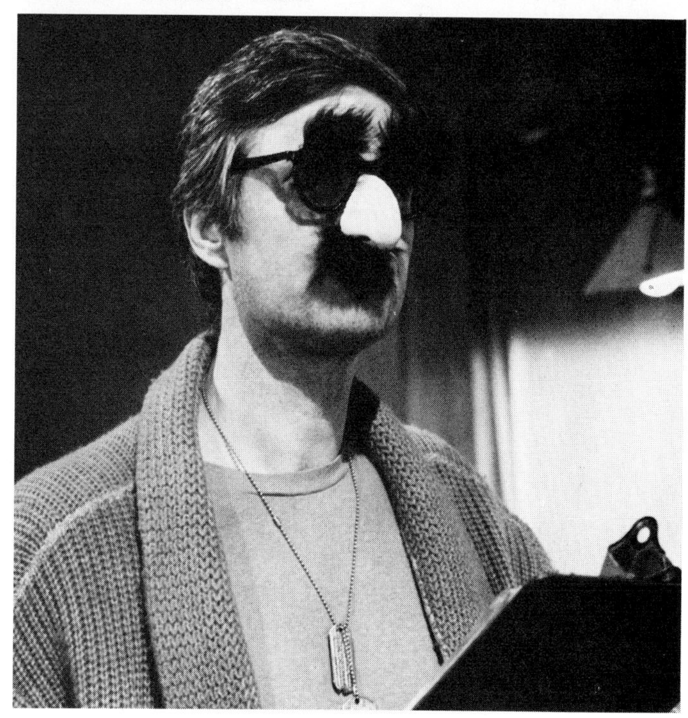

Alan makes like a Harlem Globetrotter.

Alan and Mike horse around while A

while he was still in college. Arlene, a talented musician, was playing the clarinet. The Aldas have lived in the same town in New Jersey for 17 years. Alan did not want to give up his family's roots there for his career and would fly home each weekend six months of every year. Alan never found the long-distance commutation particularly onerous and, in fact, got a considerable quantity of writing done on those trips.

Alan bristles a bit at the suggestion that he is thought of as the stereotypical "nice guy." He feels that "nice guy" carries a connotation of weakness, a person who will take all kinds of abuse from others and not say what he thinks. "Fair but aggressive" is the way Alan thinks of himself, and saying what he thinks is a way of life for him. "One of the things I'm pleased with myself for is that I've grown to be a person who will tell somebody, if they're standing on my toe, to kindly get off. And, if they don't get off," he says firmly, "I'll help them off."

He doesn't enjoy having anybody take advantage of him and will take action when it's necessary. "I love a good lawsuit," he says. "However, I don't get into one unless I think I can win. In the past, once or twice, people have attempted to take advantage of me in business because they thought I was a 'nice guy' and wouldn't complain, and I've sued the pants off them and won. I love it because I enjoy sticking up for myself. In some ways Hawkeye and I are alike in that regard."

Alan Alda is regarded primarily as a comic actor, but he has played a good deal of drama during his long career. He gravitates, however, to the opinion that comedy is more difficult than drama and by way of illustration cites the famous theater story that M*A*S*H's Harry Morgan tells about a dying actor. The actor's last words are, "It's hard to die." Then the actor pauses and says, "But comedy is harder." Comedy is a delicate technique that often requires the actor to be faithful to the specific

stant Rosemary Chiaverini looks on.

words, the sound of the words, and the rhythm of the words the writer has chosen in order to get the laugh.

Alan speaks of Larry Gelbart, one of the original writers and creators of M*A*S*H, with great respect. "Larry Gelbart's writing is excellent training for an actor because it almost always has a strong, underlying passion, but the words have to be acted absolutely precisely because they're very carefully chosen. He often writes a kind of comic poetry. There's a great deal of attention that has to be paid to technique and simply getting the words out in the right way. And, while you're doing that, you have to make sure the character continues to appear lifelike and doesn't look like somebody who came in to deliver a speech."

The pattern that Larry Gelbart set with M*A*S*H from the beginning, of mixing comedy and drama, is one factor that has made the series last so long, Alan feels, and has made the actors content to stay with the series. Being just zany for eight seasons and never recognizing death, loneliness, despair, jealousy, or the hatred that endures in the real world would have bored the actors to distraction, and they are all grateful for the chance to mix the two. "It's a wonderful experience as a performer," Alan says, "to go from a very serious moment to a very light moment and sometimes switch back and forth and mix them and have one turn into the other. It's exciting for an actor to do that."

His summation of what ingredients make up an actor might well serve as lesson number one for every aspiring actor:

"Like any artist," he says, "the actor has to be open to inspiration, intuition, and the unconscious. When you know what you're looking for, that's all you get—what's previously known. But, when you're open to what's *possible,* you get something new, and that's creativity. You have to maintain a controlled environment so you can stay a responsible member of the group." Asked to complete the phrase, "An actor is a person who . . . ," Alan thinks at length and finally says ". . . uses his or her mind and body to represent human experience."

Alan reflects on mutual alma mater with writer Thad Mumford.

Since human behavior and its exploration are the raison d'être of an actor, it's only natural that the same motivation carries over to Alan's writing. He reports that he has wanted to be a writer since he was eight years old and didn't want to be an actor until he was nine. Consequently, writing is something of a first love for Alan, and he has been able to reach fulfillment of that love since appearing on the M*A*S*H series by writing many segments and winning an Emmy for his script "Inga." Winning the Emmy was one of the biggest thrills of his life, an emotion he expressed on the award show by turning a cartwheel as he went up to the dais to receive his statuette.

Alan has decided opinions about what ingredients go into making a writer. "You have to be a good observer, and you have to be willing to go past the point where it's '*okay*,' until you get to the point where it's really something special. You have to be able to abstract so you can see a whole world reflected in a very tiny portion of it. I think a writer has to like people and know people and know himself or herself pretty well."

Alan avoids messages in his writing. He claims to be mostly interested in trying to give people an opportunity to feel, to go through an emotional experience. Then, he believes, they can reconsider, in a personal way, their own behavior. In Alan's opinion there is nothing more interesting than what people *do* to one another.

Alan's award-winning script "Inga" was inspired by a personal and extremely human experience. In the course of dinner with some friends, a feminist issue was discussed and his friends disagreed with him on the subject—sharply, he felt. He thought about the discussion for days afterward because he felt uncomfortable about it, and arrived at the discovery that he actually did not feel comfortable being *disagreed* with. He took it a step further and wondered if he was having a problem learning something from women. The more he examined his feelings the more he felt there might be a good story in this.

The result was "Inga," the story of a female surgeon with greater surgical skills than Hawkeye's who challenges him in an area where he has always felt expert and superior.

It isn't surprising that Alan is aware of the rights of women. His wife Arlene is a multitalented woman, independent, and with a strong sense of self-identity. She continues with her music, practicing the piano these days on a regular basis, and is a professional photographer. Her pictures have been shown in New York galleries and published in books and magazines. Calling Arlene warm, witty, and wise sounds like a cliché, but as one friend put it, "You've only to talk to her for a minute to begin to feel that she's the most beautiful woman you've ever met. She has extraordinary charm and intelligence."

Alan is a concerned and loving father to his three daughters, Elizabeth, Beatrice, and Eve, and has kept a sharp eye out for their development as individuals. He says, "I've resisted their getting public attention simply on the basis of being my daughters. If they do something to earn attention on their own then, of course, they're entitled."

Like most writers, Alan has times when writing is difficult and painful. But when the words are flowing from him easily, he finds it as exhilarating an experience as acting. "Writing, for me, at those moments when I can somehow get deep into my unconscious and come up with something that is true and recognizable and felt—or funny—or both—in which the kernel, the nugget of real experience, is keenly felt, is wonderful."

What he means by recognizable, he explains, is not merely that something seems familiar, "but that you know you've gotten to the heart of something. The way a flower really smells, or how important it is when you're really lonely to hear a kind word. Those times when something just leaps up off the page and says, 'That's true, that's really what that part of life is really like.' It's very pleasurable to get that up out of your insides and get it down on paper so it will be coherent and meaningful to somebody else."

Writing, for Alan, is a way of being in touch with other people, a way of communicating, and it gives him enormous pleasure to know that people have laughed and cried at something he's written. Just as he feels it is more difficult to act in comedy than in drama, he feels writing comedy is harder than writing straight drama. In a drama, if *all* you are is interesting, it's okay. In comedy, if the audience is aware that you intended to be funny and you're not, you have egg on your face.

Writing for M*A*S*H requires the writer to deal with a comedy/drama mixture that Alan considers the ideal form of playwriting. He feels this reflects what life is really like—both funny and sad. "There are very few lives that are without any cheer, and there are very few lives that don't have some tragedy in them. I think the best drama has some laughter in it, and the best comedy has some places where you cry."

Mike reasons with Alan at the ranch location.

Experiencing life and writing drama came together effectively for Alda when he was working on a segment for the show entitled "Dear Sigmund." He was attempting to write a speech for Colonel Potter (Harry Morgan); in the course of the speech the colonel reads a letter that Radar (Gary Burghoff) has written to the parents of an ambulance driver who has killed himself driving his ambulance too fast. The speech turned out to be a touching moment in the show for an unusual reason. Alan wrote those lines on a night when he had stayed up until dawn because the place where he lived had just been burglarized. He was filled with rage, fear, loathing, and a feeling of violation, and somehow those feelings, though they had nothing to do with the death of an ambulance driver in Korea in 1951, produced an exploration of Radar's reaction to that death in a way Alan hadn't anticipated. Alan reflects on the scene, "I think there was more feeling in that speech than I would have had if I hadn't just been through that terrible experience." That story illuminates Alda's answer to the question put to him, "A writer is a person who . . . ?" His answer: "A writer is a person who can squeeze life into words."

Above: Alan laughs with director Charles S. Dubin.

Alan responds to a joke from father Robert Alda.

Right: Actor/director Jackie Cooper describes for Alan the action in an upcoming scene.

Left: Alan rehearses a scene in the compound.

Artists like Alan Alda are called "hyphenates" in the entertainment industry. This means he wears more than one hat professionally. He is an actor (hyphen) writer (hyphen) director. In the fifth year of the series Alan Alda added another title to his growing list—that of creative consultant. After Larry Gelbart left the show, Gene Reynolds, Burt Metcalfe, and Alan were the only three people in the creative end of the show with continuity. Writers coming in to do the show were talented and everyone had confidence in them, but they hadn't been with the show for four years as Alan had. It was felt that his participation as creative consultant was one way of maintaining the continuity, of keeping up the standards of the show.

Creative consultant is an umbrella title embracing many areas of responsibility for Alan. He works out stories with writers, polishes scripts, makes suggestions on the set as to how scenes might be improved, watches rough cuts (a version prior to the final editing), and sometimes suggests writing a new scene. As director, Alan is involved in the editing process of the show. He is firm on one point: "I don't see how a director *cannot* be involved in editing," he says. "Editing is the basic grammar of film. It's like asking a writer if he does his own punctuation, or like an actor saying, 'I'm too busy to do my own acting,' and sending in somebody who looks like him to say the lines."

Alan regrets that the network requires a laugh track on M*A*S*H and considers it a "dumb" TV convention. Executive producer Burt Metcalfe keeps the laugh track as low as possible. So low, in fact, Alan says, that people sometimes report they've watched the show for years, suddenly notice the laugh track for the first time, and are upset because they feel it's distracting. "They play it in England without the laugh track and everybody loves it. So it really isn't necessary," Alan insists.

Alan has also added to his hyphenate status a fifth and sixth title by creating and producing a series for CBS called "We'll Get By." Fellow M*A*S*H cast member David Ogden Stiers (Charles Emerson Winchester, III) attributes this aspect of the Alda career to "Alan's hyperactive, creative urge."

Much has been written about the family feeling among the M*A*S*H cast members and their off-camera camaraderie. Alan believes it is their "playfulness" that maintains their extraordinary harmony. "Mike Farrell and I play together. We play Scrabble, word games, chess, and we can't walk across the compound from the set to our chairs without Mike falling a couple of steps behind me and trying to trip me. The poor man is *obsessed* with tripping."

The most playful one of all, however, is Harry Morgan, whom Alan terms an "inspired leprechaun." "Harry rarely says anything that would be funny if you wrote it down on a piece of paper, but his pure playfulness is so contagious that we laugh with him all day long. He's a treasure."

The acting company clearly shares a feeling of affection, but they also share a strong desire to give their best to the show professionally.

Alan believes that solid entertainment values can be included in a show without doing it cheaply, without playing down to the baser tastes of the audience. In other words, that one can do physical comedy without being tasteless, mindless, and pointless. "An awful lot of the programs I see on television seem to be sticking a tube out of the set into my body and sucking the life out of me, instead of revivifying me. Good entertainment makes you feel a little bit more full of life when you finish watching it, not a little bit less."

How does M*A*S*H, operating under these same standards and pressures, manage to hold its reputation as one of the few exceptional half hours in television? Alan guesses that the answer is that the staff and cast care enough to stick with what they are doing until they get as close as possible to their very best. Over the years a basic line below which they do not allow themselves to dip has been established. That basic line represents a level of recognizable human behavior, a level of respect for people—a respect for the differences in people, Alan explains, that they struggle to maintain. He refers to a remark comedian Jack Benny once made when asked, "Why is your show always so good?" Benny replied, "I try never to do a lousy show." "Which seems like a low standard to hold," Alan laughs, "except that it's a pretty high standard when you realize there are people who don't seem to care whether they do lousy shows or not."

The creators of M*A*S*H make a deliberate effort to break new ground several times a year. They attempt to shake up the storytelling form and delight audiences with a new approach or a new and deeper look at one of the characters.

Alan feels one can make people laugh and cry superficially with almost equal ease. "But," he says, "to make people feel deeply, or make people laugh, not just in response to a verbal tickle, but to laugh deep in their heads and hearts, is very hard. It's hard to move people, not just to cry, but to recon-

Alan pauses in his direction of a scene to enjoy a moment with the children in the show.

sider their whole lives. That's hard stuff to do."

Alan is one of the most decorated actors in the history of television. He has had Emmy nominations and awards for acting, directing, and writing, and has been loaded with assorted other trophies as well. He has a People's Choice Award, Golden Globes from the Hollywood Foreign Press Association, the American Academy of Humor's Comedy Award, and Most Popular Actor of the Year Award from *Family Weekly* magazine.

Many polls and magazines have attested to Alan Alda's tremendous popularity with audiences. Probably the most important poll to a TV actor is an unacknowledged popularity list called the TVQ (TV Quotient), which is used extensively, and often unfairly, throughout the television industry by programmers and producers to choose which actors to use in order to achieve the largest possible audience. Alda is number one on this important list.

Many people are actually excluded from work because they're not rated on the TVQ, and Alan finds this unfair. "How," he asks, "do you get into that golden group of acceptable people if the audience doesn't know you because they've never seen you, and they never get to see you because you're not in that golden group?" It's one of the many Catch 22's in the entertainment industry. Does he mind heading such a list? "Anytime they have a list of people who are swell, it's nice to be at the top of it," Alda says. "However, I wouldn't feel bad if they did away with the damn thing. I don't need to be at the top of a list that keeps people out of work. I think people should be chosen on their ability."

Alda is on top of the TVQ now, but he paid his dues to get there, "including living on $45 a week from the unemployment office," he says, "driving a cab, being a doorman, selling mutual funds, being a clown at the openings of gas stations and chicken-parts stores, and coloring baby pictures. I once made $25 for being hypnotized at a psychiatric

Hawkeye reacts to Colonel Potter's phone conversation.

clinic as a subject in a study."

In those early years, Alan had to apply all his energies to earning a living because he had a wife and children, and he and his wife Arlene both worked hard to keep the family going. Alan didn't make a living at acting until he was 29. He had begun at the age of 16. By the time he was 29 his name was *over* the title, the ultimate in billing, on Broadway, and from that time on he made a good living.

He doesn't forget how difficult it was, however, to be out pounding the streets eight hours a day, visiting agents' offices and casting directors with only a couple of dollars in his pockets. He says, wonderingly, "I remember thinking that to really have a lot of money would mean I could go into any luncheonette on any street and order anything I wanted. It wasn't until I was really making a living that I could see that in perspective and realize how modest my understanding was of what it meant to have money. I would pick a luncheonette in those days and, if they had a hamburger for 85 cents, I wouldn't go in. I would go someplace where they had a hamburger for 50 cents."

And how about today? "Now I get 85-cent hamburgers," he quips. "About 10 years later I thought that to have money meant I would be able to go anywhere in the world on a moment's notice—just pick up and go." And now? He smiles and says, "Now, I think to have money would be to buy Argentina."

Artists bring large chunks of themselves to their art. In Alan's case he likes to see story characterizations that reflect some insight into people, some understanding of why people behave the way they do, some recognition that life is both good and bad.

Alan, as has been noted, is an ardent feminist. Consequently, he's interested in exploring the lives of the female characters in the same ways he explores the male characters. "I want them to be seen as people, with the same aspirations, frustrations, hopes, fears, strengths, weaknesses, human frailties, and human strengths. I have always felt that we haven't done that enough on M*A*S*H."

Some years ago Alan was on a television talk show discussing feminism. After the show he received a phone call asking if he would like to work for the Equal Rights Amendment that had been proposed a year earlier. In the half dozen years since that night Alan has worked hard for ratification of the amendment.

"There are 14 states that already have Equal Rights Amendments in their constitutions, but there are states where a married woman can't own her own house even if she's bought it herself and made all the payments, because the man owns whatever is owned in that marriage," Alda says. And he makes it clear that he doesn't want his daughters to have to shop around for a state in the Union where they can live with the same right to equality that he has merely by being a man. "It's a serious situation," he says. "The Equal Rights Amendment is an urgently needed legal document so we can have the kind of equality that we *think* we have already but, in fact, don't."

Alan's commitment to equality may stem, at least in part, from the fact that he feels he owes his life to a woman from Australia whom he never met. The woman was Sister Elizabeth Kenny, a nurse who discovered a treatment for infantile paralysis during World War I. But, as Alan points out when he tells her story, the medical profession refused to accept her findings for about 20 years, largely because they were simply not interested in hearing from a woman on the subject. After a long struggle to get her treatment accepted, she was finally invited to the United States to lecture. About two years later, when he was seven years old, Alan was stricken with polio. And her treatment, he feels, saved his life.

"She got here in the nick of time," he says. "Without her I wouldn't be here today. And it wasn't just her discovery that saved my life. It was the fact that she wouldn't take 'no' for an answer from the men who were holding her back. I think I owe my life to Sister Kenny in two ways: I owe it to a woman's inventiveness, and to a woman's own, personal victory over sexism."

So . . . the out-of-work actor pounding the streets of New York has become Alan Alda, the "hyphenate" of mind-boggling talent and productivity, and one of the most beloved all-media stars in America. He paid his dues along the way, and it may fairly be said that playing Hawkeye Pierce in this most respected of TV series, M*A*S*H, has had the most impact on the largest number of people. Alan knows very well the value he's received from the experience: "It's been a time of growth for every single one of us, artistically and personally. We're all stronger and more interesting people than we were when we started. We're all tremendously grateful for it. It's bigger than all of us and I don't think anybody will ever understand quite why—except that maybe it gets to the heart of existence—the utter caring in the face of utter brutality. You could explore that for a thousand years and never get to the bottom of it. We've been given the opportunity to bring everything we can to it, all our experience and our skill and our art and our craft. It's been a wonderful opportunity."

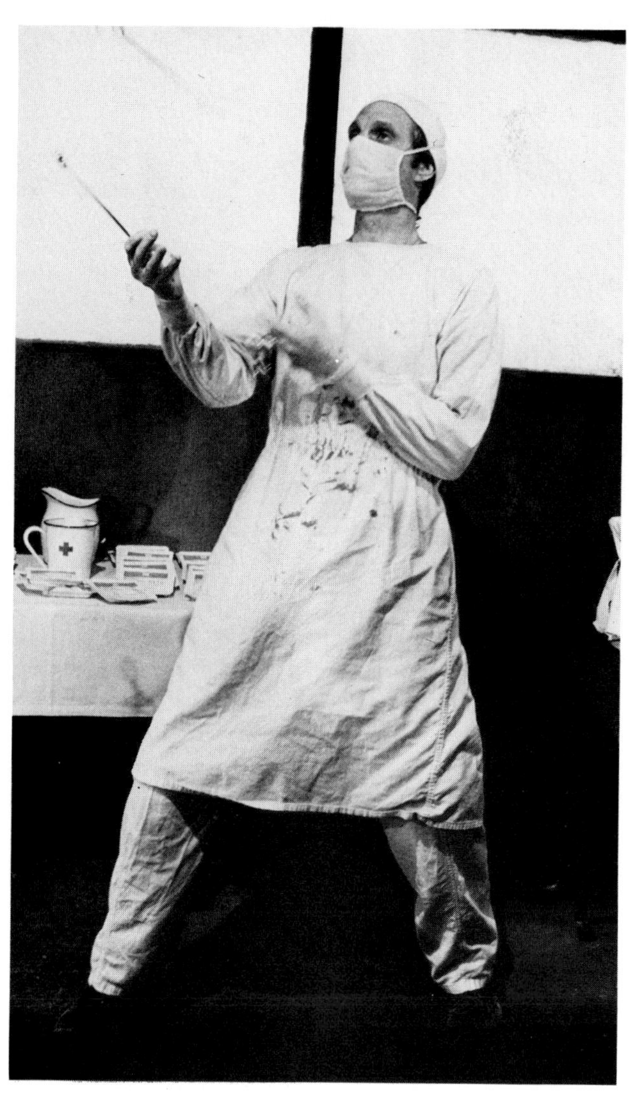

Alan "on guard" for an operating room scene.

Gary Burghoff

Approached on the last day he played Corporal Radar O'Reilly on M*A*S*H, Gary Burghoff was exhausted from seven years of demanding work. When asked to comment on the character he played and the M*A*S*H experience in general, he said, tiredly, "Ask me again in a year or two."

A year and a half later a happy, rested Gary Burghoff apologized for his inability to express himself on the earlier occasion, saying, "I was so tired after seven years, I didn't know *what* my perceptions were. That last year I was sometimes irritable, sometimes happy—but *all* the time, tired."

Gary loved and appreciated his years on M*A*S*H but found that the exposure on television changed his life incredibly—and for the worse in one important way. "Anyone who thinks being recognized on the street 24 hours a day is a pleasant experience may have a serious surprise coming, because," he says, "it can be a pain. Everyone you meet, even potential friends, relates to you as the character you play, and you begin to wonder whatever happened to the guy you were. I began to wonder if there was a Gary—just a simple Gary. That is not the M*A*S*H experience only, you understand; it's just what happens in series television."

Little more than a decade before, Gary had been a relative unknown, appearing in Off-Broadway's *You're a Good Man Charlie Brown.* Now he is among the best-known actors in America, having played (and *still* playing in re-runs on syndicated TV) one of M*A*S*H's most beloved characters. To millions of Americans, Gary Burghoff *is* Radar, the character he has invested with loyalty, sweetness, and naivete; the Andy Hardy of the 70s. Radar is champion of all creatures more helpless than himself, the perpetual adolescent struggling with pimples and sex, the patriot uncomplainingly doing his best for his country, a son idolizing his mother, and

a friend fiercely loyal to the crazy characters who people his M*A*S*H unit. He's everybody's little brother—tagging along, tugging at your jacket and asking questions, listening with open-mouthed horror, amazement, or joy to your answers, slipping in to help out before you ask, and wiggling his entire body in delight when you pat him absently in gratitude.

Gary Burghoff has obviously touched the heart of America; but, more significantly, he is appreciated by the people who have worked most closely with him on M*A*S*H.

At the 1977 Emmy Awards, Gary was the winner for best supporting actor in a comedy series for his M*A*S*H role as Radar. In announcing the winner, his M*A*S*H co-star Alan Alda, himself an Emmy champ, said that he was happy Gary wasn't on hand to accept the award in person. The reason, Alda explained, was that "It gives me an opportunity to tell the world what a wonderful, gifted, and sensitive actor Gary Burghoff is—something he, of course, would not say about himself."

The public doesn't think of Gary Burghoff as a musician, but the fact is that music has been a large part of Gary's life since he was a high-school sophomore in Delavan, Wisconsin. He joined a local orchestra as a drummer, singer, and entertainer, and appeared regularly in Milwaukee clubs.

Upon leaving school Gary took his already well developed talents and made the traditional pilgrimage to New York City. Following the path of most young actors, he sold underwear at Saks Fifth Avenue while studying acting with Sandy Meisner, James Tuttle, and Charles Nelson Reilly. In his off-time, he formed his own musical group, "The We Three Trio," which achieved moderate success and helped him showcase his musical talents. He sang at such good night spots as The Duplex and the Nag's Head Inn, acted at the best regional theaters, including New Haven's Long Wharf (as an apprentice actor) and the Rochester Music Theatre in Rochester, New Hampshire. He broke into television with appearances in "Repertoire Workshop," the "Today" show, and on PBS in "An Evening's Journey to Conway, Mass." He did TV commercials, cut a few records, and found time to write a number of songs. (Gary has written more than 100 songs and has been a three-time winner of the ASCAP Award for Excellence.)

Fortune at last ran strongly in Gary's direction, and in March 1967, he opened Off-Broadway as the original Charlie Brown in *You're A Good Man Charlie Brown*. The show ran nearly a year there before moving to Los Angeles for a successful engagement that flung Gary Burghoff straight into the arms of fate. Film director Robert Altman, hearing of Gary's work in the show, cast him as Radar O'Reilly in the spectacularly successful feature film M*A*S*H.

When asked if he found it difficult to make the transition from the film to the television series, Gary says, "I don't really feel there was a transition, although I did have to re-create the Radar character because he wasn't fully developed in the feature. He was subliminal and so little used and seen in the feature that I really had to create a new character for the TV show. The only thing that stayed basically the same was the clothes."

Gary perceives the film version of Radar as somewhat of a sardonic little guy, while the character in the television show is kindhearted and naive.

For his re-creation of the character, Gary gives a large portion of the credit to creative executive Larry Gelbart. Gelbart did with Radar what he ultimately did with all the continuing M*A*S*H characters, which was to observe the actors and base the writing of their characters more and more on the actors themselves. As all human beings are unique personalities who change and grow, Gelbart reasoned that this approach would insure the uniqueness, growth, and change of the characters he was writing about. In Gary's case, he watched him on the set and used Gary's habit of occasionally mispronouncing words, his penchant for getting his back up when he thought someone was poking fun at him, his kindness toward animals, and his real feeling for nature. He understood something of Gary's simple family background, his Connecticut/Wisconsin upbringing, his need for acceptance and love, and he wrote them into the scripts as part of Radar's persona.

In creating the character of Radar, Gary looked for a void to fill, a way to be different from the other cast members. He saw a group of sophisticated, worldlywise adults, and decided *he* was not going to be worldlywise or very adult.

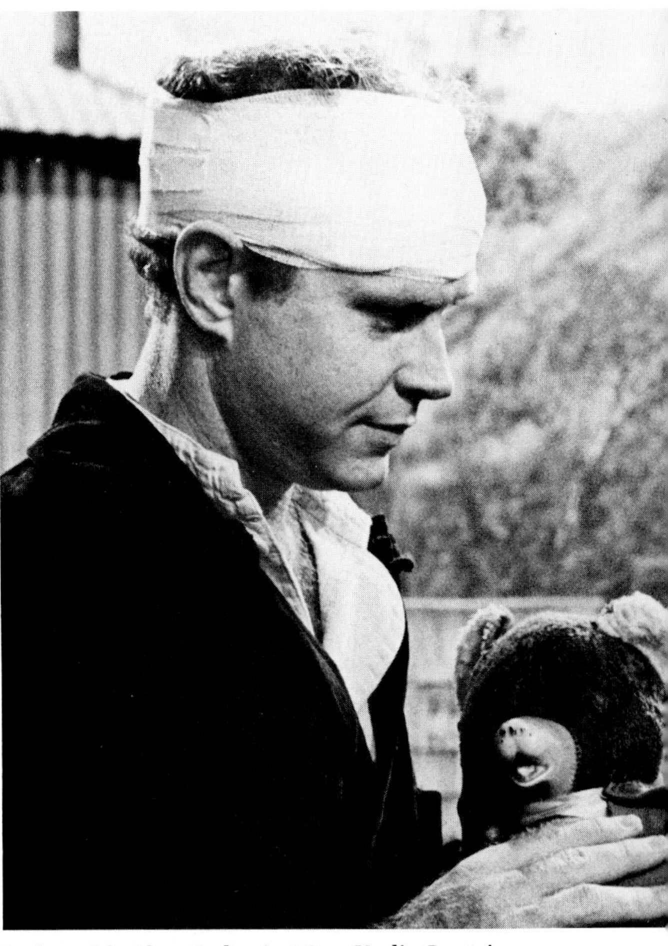

Radar with Alan Fudge in "Quo Vadis Captain Chandler?" episode.

He made another important early decision. "I made the firm determination that no matter when the camera was on me, I was going to do something interesting. Not necessarily funny, but interesting." That was what Larry Gelbart was seeing on the screen for the first three seasons—those little, interesting things. Gelbart picked up on them and enlarged them and worked on them with Gary. They were things that were coming out of what was going on in the scene. People have said to Gary, on occasion, that he's the best listener around as an actor. In actuality, that was the way he had decided to build the character—as someone who listens to everything, not only with his ears but with his heart. Radar felt things intuitively.

The danger for the actor who plays one character for many years, aside from the obvious ones of becoming stale and being stereotyped, is the limita-

Patching through a call.

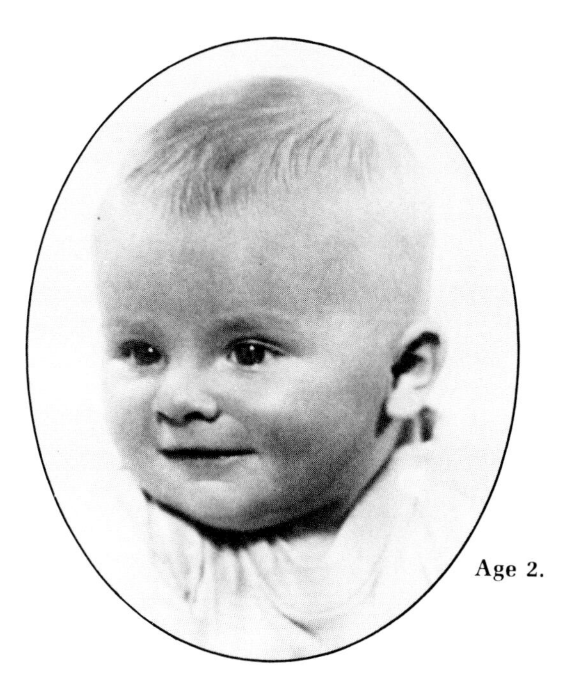

Age 2.

Caught in sniper fire.

tion on the growth of the character that actor plays. For a sensitive and dedicated actor like Gary, this problem causes enormous frustration. "Characters can't really grow up. They're frozen in time. You can't have a character actually growing like real human beings do." He beats his fist on his knees in exasperation. "Korea took place over two years. Well, we've been doing it for several times that much and you want to *let life go on*. You want to let people grow *up*. I went from 28 years old to 36 years old in this series, and I was *still* playing an 18-year-old kid."

Radar has grown in that he's been wounded and had his first love, but these are more like events than real growth. The problem is that the segments go immediately into syndication and are shown out of order, and any progressive growth on the part of the character is impossible. It has to be, therefore, momentary growth, then back to being the same person for the next episode. Gary says, "There's something false about it that has always bothered me. But that's not about M*A*S*H, that's about television."

Actors have various ways of combating this necessary lack of depth and dimension in their characters. Gary remembers asking Larry Gelbart to give Radar a first name, because the cute nickname just wasn't full enough. He felt a real name would give him a feeling of more richness within his character. That, in turn, gave Gelbart the idea of giving Radar a real family, which led to some memorable moments where Gary played Radar's mother in home movies.

The slightly surreal time problem—two years of Korea versus eight years of M*A*S*H—has actually worked in the series' favor in one way. There have been many cast changes during the first eight years, and M*A*S*H has survived the changes smoothly and without losing popularity because the show was more believable *as the result of* the changes. As Gary says: "M*A*S*H is the perfect vehicle for that. Nobody stayed in Korea forever. Even MacArthur didn't stay there for eight years. People come and go, and the show lent itself very well to that. In fact, the changes helped."

Everyone seems to agree, in any case, that M*A*S*H is no *one* person. M*A*S*H is a concept, an ensemble effort. With the possible exception of Hawkeye, no one character is irreplaceable. Many people have said to Gary, "Gee, how can you leave M*A*S*H? You're the only reason I tune in." Gary refuses to believe that. "I think they're going

Radar considers advice from Hawkeye.

Radar and pal.

to tune in anyway, because M*A*S*H is the star of M*A*S*H. No one person leaving is going to change that. The M*A*S*H experience is not so much Hawkeye, B.J., Radar, Hot Lips, and the rest as it is a curious and real statement about life and the experience of Korea."

The M*A*S*H family is like any family unit, Gary says, in that there is a tremendous bond of love, but there are also problems. He says, however, that the problems "last about a minute." Harry Morgan is the person to whom Gary is closest and the one with whom he keeps in the most constant contact. "My own father passed away this year," Gary says softly. "I think of Harry as my new father."

Of Alan Alda, Gary says, "Alan is the most incredible worker and creator I've ever met. I am bowled over by his talent and his energy."

Gary feels that Loretta Swit is the most professional actress he has ever worked with. "She always knows her lines, her timing is superb, and you can

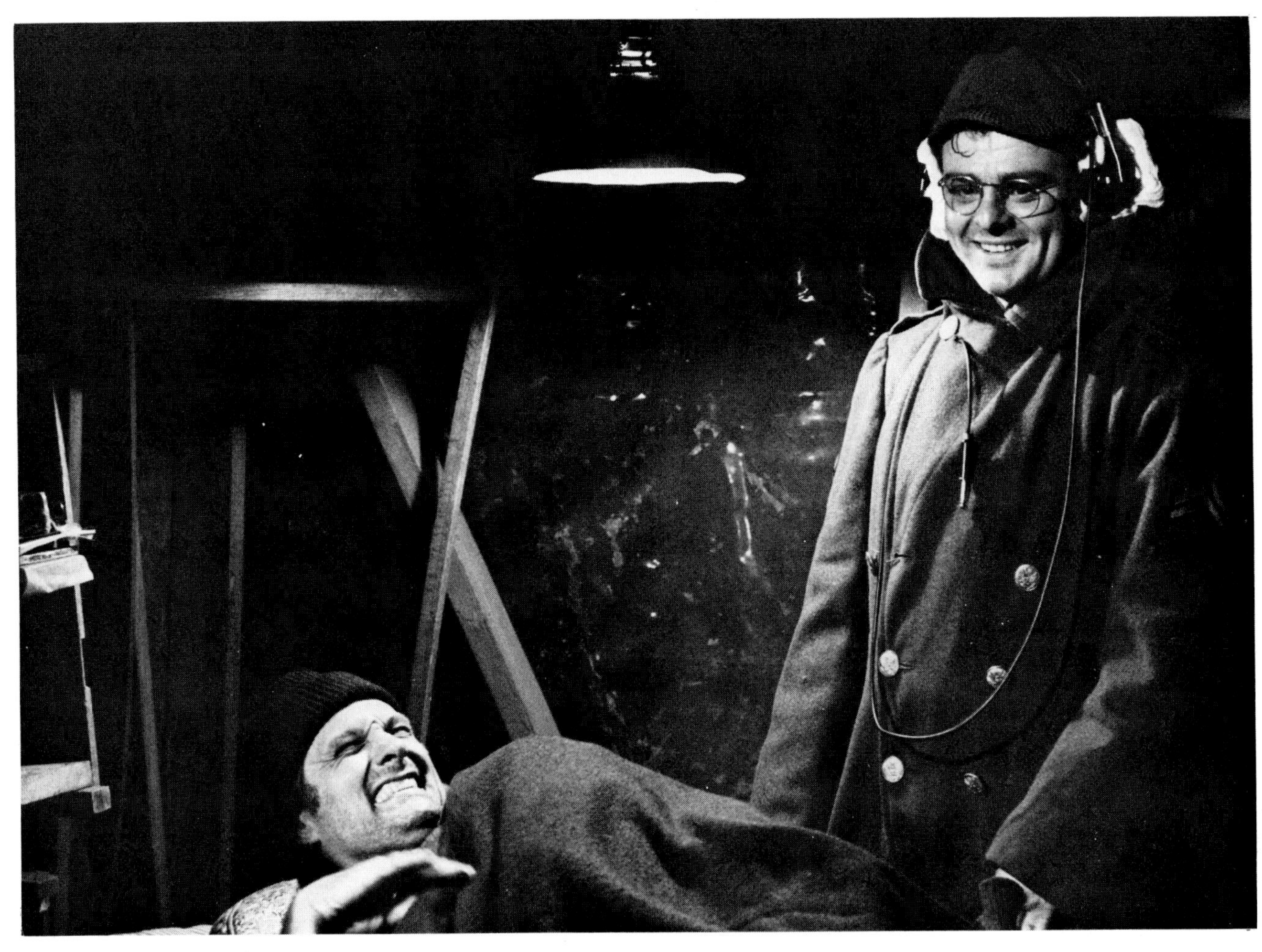

Gary and Alan during a rehearsal.

always depend on her." She was also the person he most enjoyed doing scenes with. The two characters, Radar and Hot Lips, are direct opposites, and Gary feels Hot Lips doesn't understand Radar *at all*. He's naive about sex, and she's paranoid about it. He loves to smell her perfume—that's all he needs to get turned on—but she thinks that when he looks at her he's having sexual fantasies. Gary finds that dichotomy terribly funny and enormous fun to play as an actor.

Gary reveals that McLean Stevenson kept him doubled up with laughter and wrapped in warmth for three years. He was deeply moved by the departure of McLean and by the episode that related the death of McLean's character, Henry Blake. "The scene where I brought in the message that Henry Blake had died was highly emotional for me. McLean was on the stage, and I knew that it would be the last time I would work with him. That's one of the reasons I was very full when I acted it—because it *was* real. I was going to miss McLean very much. We had worked very closely together."

Gary continues his capsule assessments of his M*A*S*H family with his admiration for Larry Linville. "He is the exact opposite of the character of Frank Burns and one of the most interesting actors I've ever met. He could discuss, knowledgeably, anything from the Great Pyramids to designing your own airplane."

Bill Christopher (Father Mulcahy), Gary terms "one of the most genuinely sensitive people and finest comedians" in his experience. "He is the kind of character actor I *love* to watch at work."

Of Jamie Farr, Gary says, "He is the kind of man who never loses his sense of reality. He will always remain a close friend."

Wayne Rogers (Trapper John) is one of the "realest" people Gary ever met. "He can be a big star and still be really himself. I learned a lot from him."

"Mike Farrell (B.J. Hunnicut) is one of the best parents I can imagine," Gary says. "He taught me a great deal about how to be a parent to my own child." Gary offers this example of Mike's attitude toward parenting: A guest actor on the set caught sight of Mike with his two children—Mike was obviously babysitting. The actor walked over to Mike, smiled, and said, "Lost the toss, eh?" meaning that Mike, instead of his wife, was stuck with the kids. Mike looked up and, without batting an eye, said, "Nope, *won* it." Gary smiles admiringly, "That's Mike."

Gary quickly pinpoints his feelings for the three executives responsible for sitting at the helm of M*A*S*H over the years. Of original producer Gene Reynolds, he says, "Gene gave me my biggest break in asking me to do M*A*S*H and gave me arm-around-the-shoulder support when I didn't win the Emmy Award the first time. I'll never forget that." About present producer Burt Metcalfe, he says, "Burt is another guy you can sit down and talk to about anything. I *like* him." Original co-producer and writer Larry Gelbart gets Gary's highest accolade: "He's a real friend and a creative genius. More than anybody he is responsible for the reality of M*A*S*H. I admire him over all other artists in Hollywood."

A large store of warmth is reserved for the crew of M*A*S*H—in Gary's opinion, the most important element on the set. He says, "With all the ballyhoo, the stardom, the press trying to turn you into a minor god, all you had to do was sit down and play a hand of poker with the crew to get brought right back down to earth—back to being 'real people.' I'm eternally grateful for that."

When a cast works closely together day after day, year after year, memorable stories often result. One of Gary's favorites involved a practical joke played on David Ogden Stiers when he was a new member of the cast. (What nobody knew at the time was that David Ogden Stiers is himself a master of the practical joke.) The cast was eating lunch in the studio commissary one day when the acclaimed British actor/director Sir Richard Attenborough entered. Stiers noticed that the cast was highly impressed and craning their necks to look at Attenborough. Stiers promptly sent a round of desserts to the M*A*S*H table with a complimentary note signed with Attenborough's name. The cast, thrilled and flattered, began waving and signaling at the bewildered Britisher, who had no idea, of course, why all these maniacs were mouthing "Thank you" in his direction. Mike Farrell finally spotted Stiers doubled up with laughter and figured, correctly, that they'd been *had*, and took revenge by sending the $40 lunch tab to Stiers. David, not to be topped, signed the bill, but with the name of Burghoff—who wasn't even there.

The next day Stiers, thrilled with his joke and wanting to take it another step, enlisted Gary in a further ploy. Gary was to pretend to be angry because his name had been signed to the check, and he and Stiers were to fake a fight. But Gary let the cast in on the joke. When Stiers returned to the set, Gary and Mike were engaged in a terrifyingly realistic fist fight, with Mike pretending to beat Gary to a pulp behind a curtain. Poor Stiers, completely convinced, was left absolutely mortified, dumbfounded, and completely vulnerable—

Radar playing his heart out.

When Gary finished the seventh season, his last, the cast had his hat bronzed and presented it to him in a farewell ceremony.

something no one in the cast had ever seen before.

Gary adds a tag to the story: "The funniest thing to me was the comment from David Hawks, our assistant director, who was not in on the gag, when he heard me being beaten up behind the curtain. He turned to the director and said, 'Gee, shouldn't we *do* something about that?'"

That event was thought to be so funny by the cast and producers that for the next season the entire episode was turned into a show dealing with a practical joke that snowballs.

Unique problems arise for any actor involved in a long-running series of any sort—problems like losing objectivity and being stereotyped. Gary has had to deal with both. He is strong in his belief that it's vitally important to have people around who will support you when you're good and tell you when you're bad. He remembers that, at one point, Loretta Swit told him that his character was getting "too cute." Gary made swift adjustments and feels tremendous appreciation for that criticism, since cuteness was something he wanted to avoid. He didn't mind if the audience thought he was cute—but he didn't want to *be* cute.

Gary was fearful when he first left M*A*S*H that he would be stereotyped as Radar and could never shake the character. He was able to provide an almost immediate antidote to the problem. He has just completed a tour of five theaters doing the hit play *The Owl and the Pussycat*. He is feeling on top of the world because he broke four of the five theaters' attendance records, and the audience, he says, left the theater feeling that he *was* Fred, the character in the play, *not* Radar in M*A*S*H.

"I'm really in a wonderful, enviable position right now," Gary says. He has a Dixieland jazz album coming out soon (on which he plays drums and sings), and he could do seven or eight weeks of theater each year and make a very fine living. That leaves the rest of the year to discover "hidden desires and talents," enjoy his family, play the drums, paint, go fishing, and indulge his abiding passion for nature and ailing seabirds. This last has earned him a reputation as "The Birdman of Malibu."

All these pleasurable forms of self-expression were put aside for most of Gary's 36 years in order for him to attain his goal of being a successful actor. They continued to be put aside while he carried the heavy work load a television series demands. There are few people who can do much else when they're doing a television series. The tendency is to eat, sleep, and drink it and allow it to become your only creative identity. The actor is in danger of denying himself his full measure of life experience. Gary says, "M*A*S*H was important to my human experience, but it wasn't the only thing I needed. TV can devour you."

Being on a television series was the most difficult situation that Gary had experienced in his entire career, because of the regimentation. "I'm not a very regimented person," Gary says, "and the repetition was awful." He actually caught himself once, while swimming in his own pool, stopping mid-stroke when an airplane flew over. [All action stops on a set when an unexpected noise is heard, because the shot is automatically ruined. The actors know the shot will have to be done again so they just stop dead in mid-action.] "The repetitiveness finally began to wear me down, and I became exhausted after seven years. People think I left M*A*S*H because I had had a bad experience. That's not true. I left because I had learned all that M*A*S*H had to teach me and I had to go on. Otherwise, you're just staying for the money. I just thank God that M*A*S*H was there for me to do. The material was of a very high order, and it was like going to school as an actor."

The only thing Gary regrets about his M*A*S*H experience is that he "fretted so much" in his impatient attempts at perfectionism. "I should have done," he says, "what I heard once in a song lyric—learned to roll like a stone. I should have had more patience, more faith that a scene would turn out okay. My sort of perfectionism made everything harder for me, exhausted me. In fact," Gary says, frowning with seeming impatience, "my work was *less* perfect because I was such a perfectionist. Having high ideals is fine, but bogging yourself down in details and losing sight of the great priorities is undercutting yourself."

Gary's greatest joy is to return to the hills of Connecticut where he is surrounded by family, and happy childhood memories are aroused by the sound of blue jays, the changes of season, and the humor and independence of the natives. "It's good," Gary laughs, "now and then, to see someone spitting tobacco." The only snake in this particular Eden is his own fame. "When you get to the homier places—places that are closer to your own roots, people carry on so much over you that you want to crawl in a hole. I *hate* being fussed over. I'd rather have the same service at a restaurant, for instance, as everyone else, and also have the same privacy and anonymity."

Gary has wanted to be an actor since he was a child, and he has worked unceasingly toward that goal. He's delighted to have the opportunity and financial security *not* to have to set any goals—to just let life happen to him, moment by moment, and enjoy it. "If you strive against all odds to become a successful actor for so many years—if you're not careful, all you know how to do is *strive against all odds*. It's like battering your head against a stone wall. I have made that wall crumble."

Asked if he can sum up his years on M*A*S*H, Gary says, "I would just like to make the statement that, after being in that wonderful and best of all television shows ever, I am also happy and excited about living a simple life as a person, with no one to say, 'Cut!' in the same room with me—and the financial security to never have to do another TV series the rest of my life. This is a poem I wrote to sum up how I feel about having experienced M*A*S*H and not wanting to let go of it for so many years, but knowing that I had to leave, because nothing is forever, and you have to go on to different things. Not necessarily better, but different, things."

A breeze just blew across my leg.
The same breeze will never cross
  my leg again.
I can't hold on to it, I can't
  make it come back.
I can't control life in any way.
What a wonderful sense of relief
  I feel discovering this
  basic truth.
I have lost nothing.
I have gained two legs to stand on
Ready to feel a new and perhaps
  more beautiful breeze flow across
  both of them.

William Christopher

The ambience around the M*A*S*H 4077 Unit is a little reminiscent of the description actress Katharine Hepburn once gave of her family—"a group of strong individualists, arguing their point of view vociferously, offering an opinion on any and every subject, and living life on a grand and reckless scale."

In a group where everyone has a strong and snappy comeback, the gentle wit of Father Mulcahy is both a charming and a necessary dramatic balance. The M*A*S*H series has evolved as a serio-comic examination of people under stress coming to grips with their problems and their growth as human beings. The emotional turmoil of "coming to grips" among all these strong, often neurotic, characters tends to be overwhelming—and *loud*. The adaptability, cheerfulness, and quiet soul-searching of Father Mulcahy over the eight years of the series have been a perfect foil—and antidote—to all that noise. Bill Christopher has taken what began as a small part and turned Father Mulcahy into one of the series' most beloved characters.

Bill reminds one greatly of what Father Mulcahy would be like if he had decided to stop being a priest and had settled down with a wife and two children in Pasadena, California. Bill has the same gentle quietness and the same way of suddenly glancing up from a book he's reading in the corner and making a comment—whether profound or funny—that stops people in their tracks. A seeking mind and a knack for cutting through complexities to the heart of the subject add to the similarities of the man and his character. He is something of a scholar and, cherishing things classical, has taught himself Latin and Greek and is lovingly restoring his old home in staid and social Pasadena. He is obviously fascinated by life and the world around him and has become a good neighbor-activist in community affairs. He is a kind and considerate

husband to his wife of 22 years and tender with his two sons—altogether a very satisfactory sort of alter ego for Father Mulcahy.

Bill was born the second of three sons to Wallace S. and Louise Christopher on October 20 in Evanston, Illinois. He broke his leg while attending both the first and second grades, and figured he was inspired to pursue an acting career when he took the part of "Ilgamood the Groundhog" in a third-grade play. "Perhaps," he surmises, "because that was the first year I didn't break my leg."

Like many fellow actors, Bill knocked on many doors, but his door-pounding covered a variety of endeavors. He was a door-to-door salesman peddling Christmas wreaths, soft-water gadgets, salves and ointments, doughnuts, souvenirs, and cowbells. Specifically, he traces his nervous wanderings to the 18th-century silversmith Paul Revere, who was, in truth, Christopher's great, great, great, great, great uncle. Bill initially began his career as a door-to-door salesman selling eggs and, due to occasional disasters with bicycle deliveries, learned at the early age of 11 not to put all his eggs in one basket unless absolutely necessary.

After graduating from New Trier High School in Winnetka, Illinois, Bill attended Wesleyan University in Middletown, Connecticut, where, while earning a Bachelor of Arts degree, he became involved in fencing, soccer, singing with the glee club, and acting in numerous dramatic productions.

"I also got involved in several excruciatingly painful blind dates," he adds. The one non-"excruciatingly painful" date was with a silk-screen artist named Barbara O'Conner, a native of Middletown, who had been described as Bill's "soul mate" by the classmate who introduced them. This appraisal was not argued by either of them since they married soon after and remain happily married to this day.

Bill Christopher has worked in every phase of

entertainment available to an actor. He acted in the review *Beyond the Fringe* on Broadway (and in its national touring company) and in *The Hostage* Off-Broadway. He also did his stint in stock companies and in regional theater, in both classical and contemporary works. His television credits go back to, among others, "The Patty Duke Show" and "Hogan's Heroes," and regular appearances on "Gomer Pyle, USMC," "That Girl," and "Nichols." In films for TV, he appeared in "The Movie Maker" and "The Perils of Pauline" and, in feature films, *The Fortune Cookie, The Shakiest Gun in the West, With Six You Get Egg Roll,* and *Hearts of the West.* Additionally, Bill improvised comedy scenes at the Harvey Lembeck Comedy Workshop in Los Angeles that led to two appearances on "The Carol Burnett Show" and, ultimately, to his appearance in M*A*S*H.

Another actor had been cast for the role of Father Mulcahy in the M*A*S*H pilot, so Bill Christopher didn't come on the scene until the opening episode of the series. He was established in television and had worked for M*A*S*H producer Gene Reynolds before, but for some reason had not been submitted for the pilot. Bill heard that the part of Father Mulcahy was being recast (after the pilot) and was duly excited when his agent told him he was to go in for an interview. He almost blew the whole thing at the first interview, however. Bill had had a great deal of experience at improvisation and, at the interview with the production staff (Gene Reynolds, Larry Gelbart, and Burt Metcalfe), decided to improvise the lines instead of reading them as written. "Actually, I improvised something because I felt that would put me more at ease and might get some interesting results," he remembers. He didn't know, at that stage, about Reynolds' and Gelbart's penchant for wanting their words read *exactly* as written.

Bill went home after the audition feeling very strongly that the role would be a wonderful one, but after several days he still had not heard from the producers. He finally got a call from Burt Metcalfe, who told him, "We'd like to have you come back. We think you certainly have some qualities that would be good for this role. However, I want to tell you one thing: we're going to have you back—not *because* of your improvisation, but *in spite* of your improvisation."

Bill's reply was a typically mild, "Oh, I see, I see," and he thought to himself, "Well, in that case, I guess they would like to hear the words that they have written." He went in for another reading, did the scene word for word, and was signed for the part the next day.

Early in the life of M*A*S*H, the character of Father Mulcahy was underdeveloped and only used in approximately half of the episodes. Over the years he has evolved, however, and has become a far more active and serious character. Bill likes doing comedy and sees Mulcahy as a comic character, but unlike the glib comedy of Hawkeye and B.J., or the lampooned pomposity of Charles Winchester, or the naivete of Radar. "To me," Bill says, "Mulcahy is a pretty straight guy who doesn't quite have a handle on everything, and there's a little bit of 'fumfing' [a favorite word of Bill's] and confusion."

Father Mulcahy is called upon to perform the services of a spiritual leader. Often, however, his office is a bit peripheral—not because of the story line, but because most of the characters don't go to church. Mulcahy's life seems to be feast or famine. At times he's overburdened and overworked, and at other times he has leisure because no one comes to him for aid or advice.

Father Mulcahy may be gentle and at times bumbling, but his basic security and intuition can occasionally cause him to go roaring forth like a lion, especially if he's riled up over something. In one episode, Mulcahy, who is a boxer, is in a bad mood because he hasn't received his promotion to captain. He is in the midst of taking out his anger on a punching bag when Klinger comes to him for help in trying to stop a fight between a Turkish and a Greek patient. The Father, effective in his anger, goes right to the heart of the matter and tells the two combatants to "knock it off" or he'll clobber them. At this point Bill smiles pontifically and says, tongue very firmly in cheek, "There is *some* precedent in the Bible for people getting clobbered who have transgressed."

Mulcahy also once stole a truck full of penicillin from some black market thugs, and he performed an emergency tracheotomy when there was no one else to do it. Bill Christopher sums up his character as adaptable. "Mulcahy has become used to the operating room and has even learned a bit of surgery. He once got sick in an early show, but now he's evolved to the point where he can go through operations and stick his hands inside people, and he's become rather interested in doing it. If there's not a job for him, he'll find one."

Each member of the M*A*S*H cast has a moment he or she remembers with special fondness. Bill's favorite moment came after he and Alan Alda had been doing a scene that Alda had written and was

Mulcahy being interviewed by Clete Roberts in "The Interview" episode.

directing. The scene between Father Mulcahy and Hawkeye was difficult and intense, and it was late when they finally finished. "We left and walked back to our dressing rooms together," Bill says. "It was dark, and we were walking under the night's sky taking a breath of the fresh air. I was quite intense, talking about some detail that was related to the work we had been doing. Suddenly Alan said, 'Oh, isn't this fun? Isn't this great! Don't you love this? This is wonderful! Isn't this fun?'"

Bill's usual quiet, measured manner changes to warm excitement as he recalls the Alan Alda of that night. "It's really wonderful to be able to work with somebody who's pretty much the star of the show, the director of the episode, the writer of the episode, and the one who's having a ball doing it. I think that's really fun. I loved working and I loved Alan's boyishness. That was a moment I really enjoyed."

He's also enjoyed being the butt of a gentle practical joke on occasion. Bill was forced to leave the show for eight weeks once due to a bout of hepatitis. When he returned he found that his chair on the set had been painted yellow. He says, "They painted it yellow because *I'd* been yellow. I thought that was very nice of them—to fix me a special chair."

There seems to be general agreement among critics, public, and the cast of M*A*S*H that the show's phenomenal success has been due, in part, to the care and quality tendered by everyone from the top down, and to the increasing emphasis on

Age 3.

the struggles of the characters to remain human in the midst of war. Bill has found his own definition. "Let's start with the words 'human value.' M*A*S*H uses these human values in many different ways. We have a format that allows us to take these human values and relationships and stretch them back and forth in different designs over and over again in new plots."

Bill Christopher's own personal "human values" have to do with his dedication to his wife and children and to service in his community. He enjoys living in Pasadena and has made it clear to his neighbors that he is civically inclined. He unselfishly makes himself available to causes, serving, for example, as a fund-raiser for the rape hotline in Pasadena, a project he considers extremely important.

One of several devoted family men on M*A*S*H, Bill leads a fairly normal life and takes his kids to ball games and Disneyland. Edward, his 11-year-old son, has been diagnosed as autistic and is being treated, as an extension patient, by the Institute for the Achievement of Human Potential in Philadelphia. He is engaged in a new therapy program that Bill says is "the first program we've encountered which has something we can believe in." It is a program in which they will be heavily involved for the next five years. John, their 13-year-old, is a good athlete. Bill says, "You've only got so many years when your children are growing up and you give them what you can. You feel that after a few years your chances of influencing them are over and they go away. Then there's just the two of you again." He stops and glances at Barbara, who is looking at him from the other side of the room. "That's going to be swell when it happens," he says, "but right now we're very much family people."

Mulcahy prepares to assist with surgery.

Bill caught deep in thought.

Jamie Farr

Corporal Klinger, as played by Jamie Farr, is the charming hustler found on the streets of any big city, the draftee who is figuring ways to con his way out of the army even as he enters the induction center. He is as inventive and crafty as most survivors of big city ghettos, and as grimly determined to find a way out of a war and an army he wants no part of.

By some quirk of character, some street code of honor, Klinger finds a dishonorable discharge unacceptable. A Section Eight (indicating mental instability), however, *is* honorable in Klinger's book. But how does he *prove* that he's crazy enough to qualify for a Section Eight? By wearing women's clothing at all times, *that's* how.

The Klingers of this world are likely to consider themselves "outsiders," scratching and scrambling to get what they figure they deserve. If they get it, and *if* they don't get tossed into jail or the stockade, it's because they're likable, amusing, sometimes brave, energetic, have a personal code of honor and, in the case of Corporal Max Klinger, add a zany entertainment factor and necessary morale boost to the beleaguered personnel of the M*A*S*H 4077 Unit.

Jamie Farr says of Klinger, "I think he's necessary for the morale of the M*A*S*H unit. I think both colonels—the one McLean Stevenson played [Henry Blake] and the one that Harry Morgan plays [Sherman Potter]—wondered what he was going to do next and looked forward to it. The man is obviously a genius. He's come up with some of the *most* creative ways to get out of the army. Of course, the doctors find him terribly amusing and very inventive."

If one looks only at the Klinger of the early days of the M*A*S*H series, there is a beautifully crafted, hilarious, but one-joke character: Klinger appearing in one improbably feminine outfit after another, inventing new and more outrageous excuses for getting his discharge. Time and development of the Klinger character have given us

glimpses of what-makes-Klinger-run, the darker side of the man and of his alter ego Jamie Farr. Neither has been privileged (as most of the other M*A*S*H characters and actors were), and both character and actor were outsiders, working desperately—within a system each had learned early was *not* geared to his advantage—to get what he wanted. Jamie has experienced this frustration at every step. "In most of my life, I've been treated as an outsider, as the guy who has his hat in his hand. That even applied to M*A*S*H when I first joined the show. I was a day player [an actor hired by the day instead of working under a contract] and it took several years, even after I was under contract, to attain equality with the production company, the studio, and the network. And I'm *still* fighting for it."

Jamie Farr grew up on the streets of Toledo, Ohio, the only son of Lebanese meat cutter-grocer Samuel Farah and seamstress Jamelia Farah. Growing up on the streets taught Jamie a form of survival and not to be afraid to "mix it up with the kind of people who are really in the majority in this country."

Some of the kids Jamie grew up with didn't have enough food—so they stole it. Whatever else they needed was stolen, too. As a result, some ended their lives violently or in prison. Jamie claims he was not affected adversely by the streets. "I was never a tough guy. I was always the kid in short pants and sandals who tried to catch up with the rest. I was always the last one to be chosen for teams—and they took me out of pity."

His close-knit family environment probably saved Jamie Farr from the effects of his surroundings. His father was the passive member of the family, and Jamie saw little of him, since he worked 14 hours a day, seven days a week. His mother, a hard-working, creative middle-Eastern traditionalist, cooked and cleaned house. "I've always loved my mother's creativity and ingenuity," Jamie says. "She would always make the most of the least." His only sibling, a sister ten years older, provided Jamie with

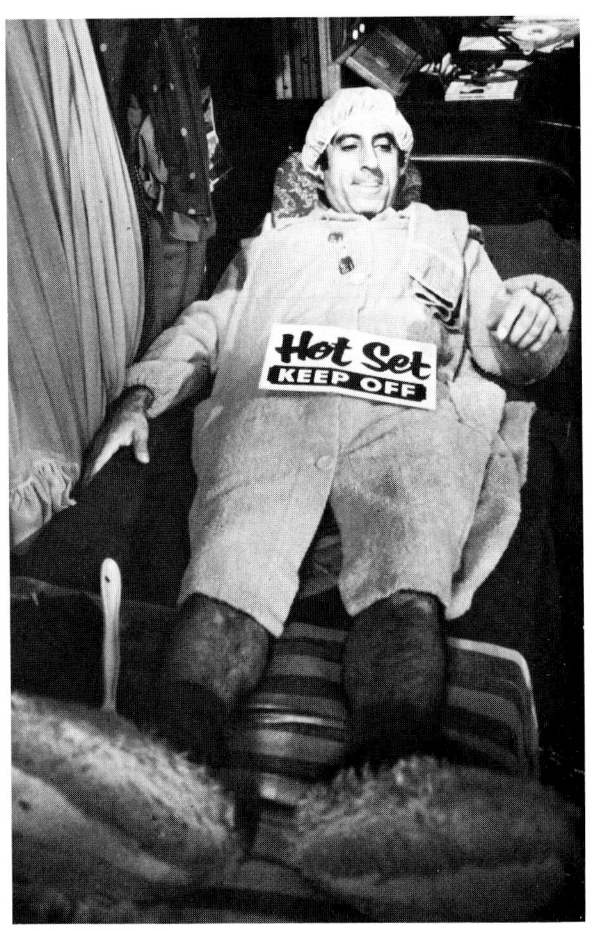

Jamie relaxes before a scene.

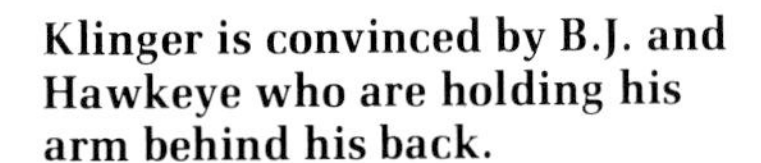

Klinger is convinced by B.J. and Hawkeye who are holding his arm behind his back.

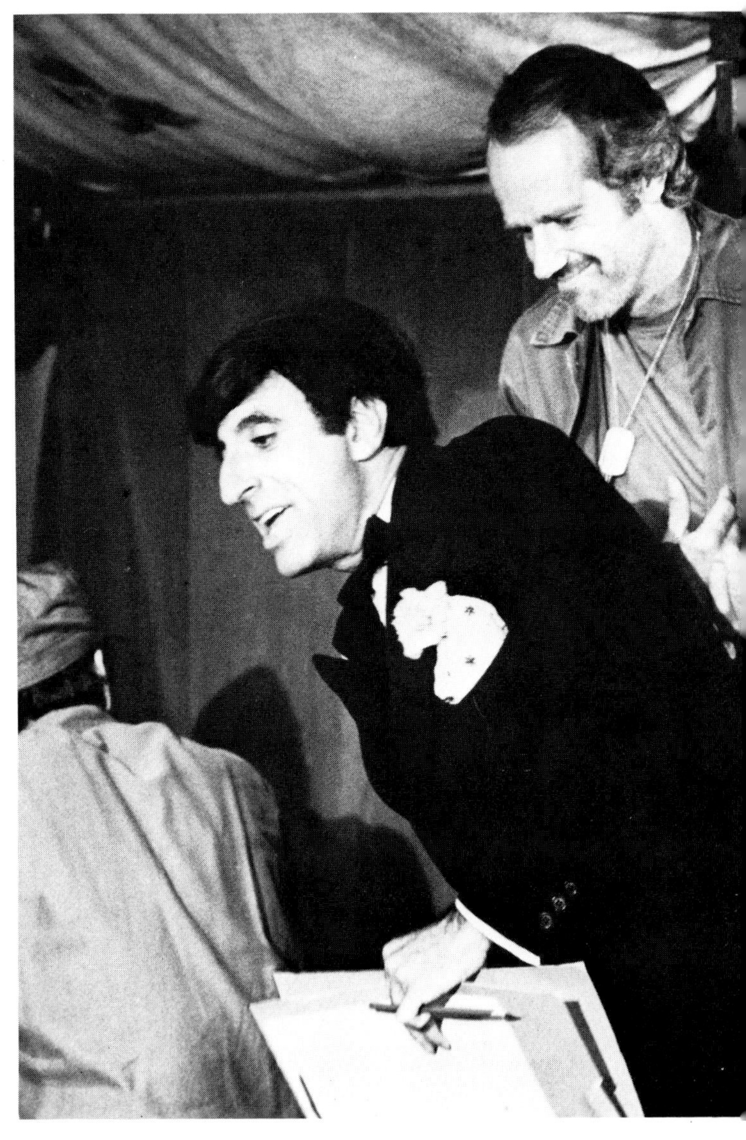

inspiration, opening his eyes to art, literature, and theater.

He was a lonely child and regrets today that he had so little time with his parents and so little personal relationship with them. Consequently, he compensates by being a pal to his own two children. "I try not to be authoritarian," he says. "I try to understand their problems and talk with them, rather than tell them what to do just because I'm the parent."

There were playmates to spare, however, on the streets of Toledo, and Jamie organized them into acting groups, re-creating all the films they saw at the local movie house. He was off and running in his acting career when he won $2 in a local talent contest. The energetic overachiever began to emerge at Woodward High School. There, Jamie was class president three years running, feature editor of the school paper, president of the radio club, manager of the football and basketball teams, star of the varsity tennis team, and a member of the drama society, writing and acting in two variety shows. Upon graduation, Jamie won the school achievement award for most outstanding student and became a member of the National Honor Society in recognition of his scholastic excellence.

After school he entered the Pasadena Playhouse, was discovered by an *MGM* talent scout, screen-tested for the successful landmark film *The Blackboard Jungle*, and won the role of the mentally handicapped student Santini. It was a big, storybook break for a young actor—an important, explosive film, the first to come out and say that the school system was not doing a good job—and his first break as an actor.

"I didn't know the first thing about professionalism until I did that film," Jamie says. "I was in an element that was totally foreign to me. I was the

Klinger tries to con Potter.

Age 2.

Klinger with Clete Roberts in "The Interview" episode.

Klinger holds an orphan.

Below right: Jamie calls a halt to the commotion.

Below: Jamie shows his affection for his hometown.

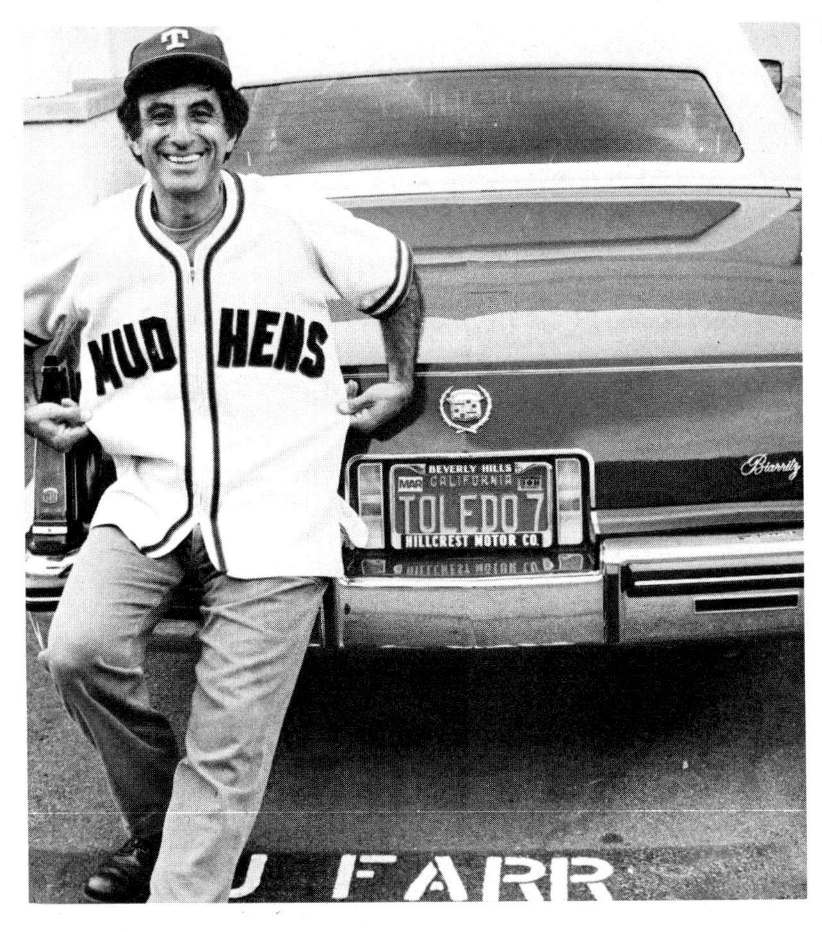

lowest paid of all the principal actors in the film, and I had to dress in a tent. I didn't even get a dressing room. There was a definite caste system and I certainly felt it."

One film does not make a career, and Jamie went back to the ranks of the unemployed actors and the real beginning of his 20-year "overnight" success story. He took all the jobs young actors take in order to eat regularly—delivery boy, post office clerk, airline reservations clerk, and "cowboy" on a chinchilla ranch. He even served his time in the army—the only member of the M*A*S*H cast who actually served in Korea. After two years, he was back in Hollywood, back to odd jobs and acting when he could find work.

In the late 1950s, Jamie became a regular on "The Red Skelton Show" at CBS, then graduated to the position of second banana with Harvey Korman on "The Danny Kaye Show." In 1971 he became a regular on "The Chicago Teddy Bears" series.

During the first season of M*A*S*H, Jamie got a call from producer Gene Reynolds to do a one-shot part playing a phony transvestite bucking for a Section Eight. He had worked for Reynolds twice before—once on "F-Troop" in which he played a stand-up comic, Indian-style, and again on "Room 222" in a scene that ended up on the cutting room floor. "I had felt bad about that, assuming I had been inadequate, and wrote a letter of apology to Gene. He promptly wrote back to say that I was not at fault—there had just been a problem with time."

When Jamie arrived on the M*A*S*H set to play the part of Klinger, there wasn't much information about the character except that he was trying to get out of the army by wearing a WAC uniform and high heels. There were only a few lines, and the director had Jamie playing Klinger with lisps and swishes—the full-fledged stereotype of a homosexual.

Gene Reynolds was appalled and made the decision to go back in and re-shoot. He called Jamie and asked how *he'd* play the part. Jamie said, "Well, I'd just play it straight, as a guy would, and forget about the fact that he's wearing dresses."

Reynolds replied, "Good, good, let's try it that way," and Corporal Klinger was launched. M*A*S*H went on to become a hit that season, and the segment that introduced Klinger, "Chief Surgeon Who?" won Larry Gelbart a Writer's Guild Award as best comedy show of the year.

Jamie was called back to play Klinger six or seven more times, joining several other minor, continuing characters being tried out during that first year. Corporal Klinger and Father Mulcahy were the only ones who made the first team.

During his own service career Jamie says he encountered a couple of characters very much like Klinger. They tried all kinds of bizarre tricks to get discharged but were generally ignored and treated with amusement. Jamie feels that it is important to remember that Klinger is a *very* good soldier who would never jeopardize the lives of any of the people around him. "Klinger is very concerned about other people—about their welfare. That's why he's a good corpsman—that's why he attends to the injured the way he does."

If an actor invests his character with many of his own personality traits, the reverse can also be true. Jamie says that he finds himself being "on the look-out" on the set for possible dangers to the cast and crew members, and trying to help if there is an injury to anyone. That's quite a switch, evidently, since Jamie claims to faint at the sight of blood. He tells of the time his mother cut her finger and sent young Jamie to get a Band-Aid. He fainted halfway to the bathroom. During his army induction physical, the drop of blood on his pricked forefinger also sent him sprawling. Jamie laughs. "I think Klinger is the new strength in me now that I'm on M*A*S*H."

Unlike Klinger, who has been married and divorced, Jamie is very happily married. In 1963 he left the location of *The Greatest Story Ever Told* in the wilds of Utah to marry model Joy Richards. He was not able to afford an engagement ring for the first 13 years of their marriage, but M*A*S*H changed all that. Jamie reflects on the tender scene. "It was really touching. We were at our favorite restaurant. The manager, who was in on the secret, made a big deal of bringing the ring [an emerald surrounded by diamonds] on a silver tray covered by a large curved top. Everyone in the restaurant thought we were celebrating our engagement." The only curiosity was their two children, Jonas Samuel and Yvonne-Rose Marie, seated at the table with them.

Jamie has mixed feelings about his success, about becoming a familiar face. "It affects you positively and negatively. Positively, it makes you famous and people know you wherever you go. Negatively, it makes you famous and people know you wherever you go!" The story is the same with most celebrities—they're grateful for the success and recognition, but it can be painful when a little privacy is needed. Jamie loves it when someone walks up and says, "Hi, Jamie, we love the show." But, to be referred to as Klinger or have people pointing at him as "that guy who wears the dresses" causes him irritation. "You work your butt off all these years—game shows, talk shows, your name's on movies, and you do whatever you can to get people to know who the hell you are, and they ask you to sign 'Klinger' as though the world won't know who Jamie Farr is. I'm an actor playing a role, and I want the audience out there to know that."

The dresses Klinger wears have been a blessing, as they have helped make the character unique. The dresses have also been a source of frustration. Early in his career on M*A*S*H, Jamie, after shooting quite late, went back to his dressing room to change. Too late he remembered he was in a dress with a back zipper and, not having experience with a back zipper, went looking for someone to get him out of this dilemma. The set was deserted. In desperation he went into a men's rest room and came face to face with a tough, macho-looking truck driver. M*A*S*H wasn't on the air yet, and the man couldn't believe what he was looking at. Jamie recalls, "Trying to explain my situation only compounded the problem, so I just asked him if he would kindly undo my dress. He was very nice and helped me out, but I got out of there as fast as I could."

As a nightclub performer, Jamie uses the role of Klinger judiciously. He does a bit of Klinger, more for the recognition factor and the expectations of the audience, then quickly packs him away and proceeds with Jamie Farr and humor based on observation.

Jamie Farr's sole hobby and interest, beyond his devotion to his family, is working. He used to write TV screenplays and pilots but considers writers to be the "doormats of the industry," and the difficulties one has to go through to sell a script "too miserable to be worth the rewards." He used to play tennis. Now he doesn't. He used to play cards. Now he doesn't. The hustling overachiever shrugs his shoulders and states, "I *enjoy* working. And, because I was out of work for so many years, I'm kind of catching up with all that inactivity."

Klinger in Toledo in the "Dreams" episode.

* Mike Farrell *

B.J. Hunnicut, as played by Mike Farrell, is the husband every woman dreams of and the friend every man wishes he had. He is compassionate doctor; faithful husband; loving father; supportive, unjudgmental friend; witty, amusing companion; and concerned humanist. He's got all the qualities with which we Americans love to invest our ideal man: honesty, integrity, honor, humor, tolerance, staunchness, and a mind of his own. He's tender with women, children, the wounded, and anyone less fortunate than himself, and he's full of quiet pride for his friends of the M*A*S*H unit as he watches their gallant struggles and their gay desperation.

Mike Farrell, who replaced Wayne Rogers as "second zany" to Alan Alda five years ago, *likes* his character B.J. In summing him up, Mike puts it this way: "He's a man of clear principles—whether or not you agree with his principles—and he maintains them."

Mike Farrell grew up in the motion-picture industry, despite being born in St. Paul, Minnesota. His father brought the four children to Southern California when Michael Joseph Farrell was two, and found work as a carpenter at a film studio. Mike went to show-bizzy Hollywood High School but never appeared in a play until after graduation from school and a two-year hitch in the marine corps. He returned from a tour of Japan and Okinawa and began to make his secret dream of being an actor come true by studying drama at Los Angeles City College and UCLA. He also studied with acting coach Jeff Corey, and with Tony Barr at the Desilu Professional Workshop.

There weren't many professional theaters around Los Angeles when Mike was beginning his career—the town was something of a cultural desert until the 70s—but he found ways to get the necessary on-stage training. He appeared in many local theater productions and trekked down to the well-regarded Laguna Beach Playhouse for such

plays as *A Thousand Clowns; Mary, Mary; Under The Yum-Yum Tree;* and *The Skin of Our Teeth.*

Eventually Mike made the break into television where he has been tremendously successful. Before M*A*S*H he starred in two television series, "The Interns" with Broderick Crawford and "The Man and The City" with Anthony Quinn. He guest-starred on such top shows as "Mannix," "The Bold Ones," "Marcus Welby, M.D.," "Owen Marshall," "Harry O," and a long list of "Movies of the Week," including *The Longest Night* with David Janssen and *The Questor Tapes* with Robert Foxworth.

Mike's film career encompasses only four films so far, but all of them were top-drawer—*Captain Newman, M.D., The Graduate, The Americanization of Emily,* and *Targets.*

When Mike started on M*A*S*H, the only thing the writers knew about the character of B.J. was that he was going to be married, have a child, and be a devoted husband, as opposed to a womanizer like Hawkeye. Mike felt the concept to be a trifle skeletal and was understandably nervous about the outcome. The usual M*A*S*H phenomenon began to happen—the writers and the actor began to flesh out the character in a totally natural and organic way. Mike's input was considerable, since he had a clear sense of the direction in which he wanted the character to go, as well as directions in which Mike Farrell just automatically *always* goes. The molding of B.J. was under way.

Mike remembers it as a bit of a fight at the beginning: "At first, it was mostly real 'straight arrow' stuff. B.J. was sort of a straight man and was in danger of becoming a bit inflexible. I kept trying to fight against that and say, 'Wait a minute, why don't we let this guy be molded by the circumstances he finds himself in? Let's curve him a little bit—have a little more fun here and a bit more willingness to round him out!' Now I grow more comfortable with him all the time. I like him more and more as he gets closer to *me.*"

But how much of Mike Farrell is in B.J., or vice

A young Mike Farrell poses with his cousin.

versa? For instance, Mike Farrell doesn't drink; he thinks he's prone to asserting himself more than B.J. is; he's a little quicker to anger, probably louder; a little coarser, and a lot more physical.

It's almost impossible for an actor to do a series on television and avoid projecting his own personality into the character. Mike's ever-lurking sense of humor took over first:

"Well, we're both tall and we have very close to the same voices, and we both have big feet, and we both have a lot of teeth. I don't know—B.J. is not me and I am not B.J. However, it's like the two of us ran at each other at high speed, collided, and what you have is what's left over."

Mike likens the ability of a wide spectrum of audience ages and types who enjoy M*A*S*H to a game of chess. If you are young you can learn the moves and enjoy the game on a very elementary level, but if you want to know the game better you can get into gambits, strategies, and patterns. M*A*S*H, he says, is appreciated in much the same way. If you want to you can just sit back and enjoy Radar and Klinger and the rest of the mob. On the other hand, people who think there is more to entertainment than sitting back and laughing can look a little deeper. And, if they look a little deeper, they will not be disappointed, he believes. There is substance to the show. It's *always* there. The audience, therefore, is a varied one.

Fame is very seductive and can take you away, literally and figuratively, from the things that are important in your life. Mike finds there's no cure for this that is as good as coming home and letting his family deflate him. One day an interviewer was at

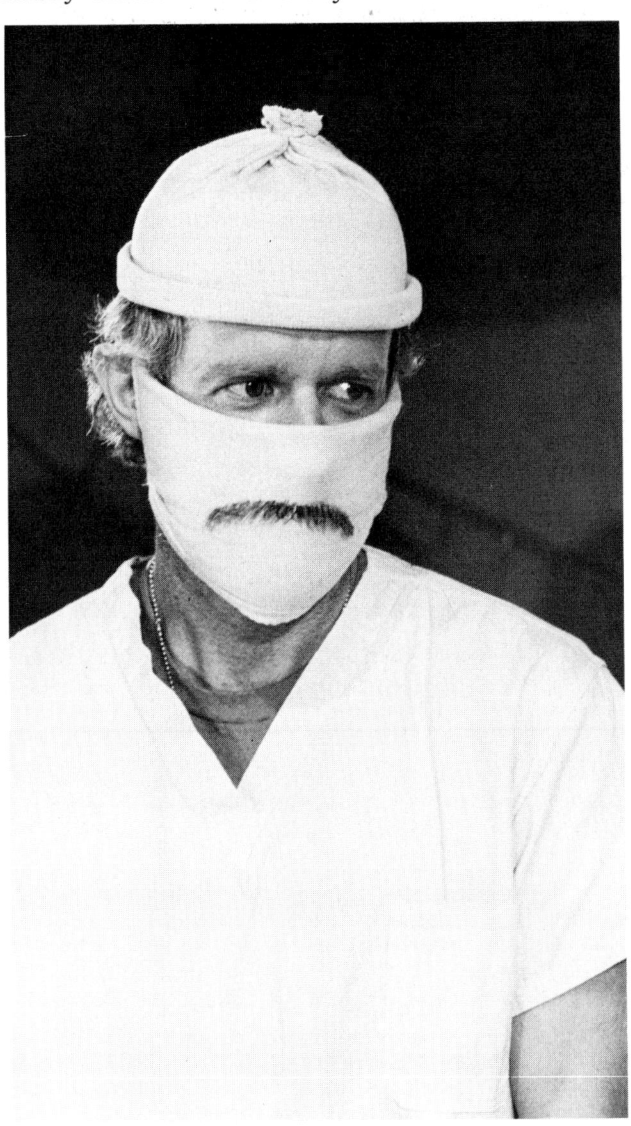

Never without his beloved moustache.

Mike carries his own weight and that of Harry Morgan.

Mike's home, asking terribly flattering questions and making him feel very important, when his little girl called out from the other room, "Daddy, I'm finished pooping. Will you come wipe me?" As Mike wryly comments, "That kind of brings you back down to ground zero, and you once again know what the absolutes are in life."

In a cast full of pranksters, Mike Farrell is considered *the* practical joker. He and Alan Alda have a close but competitive relationship—like that of brothers—and there is evidently a lot of "anything you can do, I can do better." If Mike does chin-ups, Alan will try to do one more, and if Alan does push-ups, Mike will break his back to do one more. Mike laughs when he says they used to play chess until Alda got tired of losing.

But Mike Farrell is not all fun and games. He is a serious and thoughtful man. He is serious about the causes he espouses, about his family, and about his career. He is now involved in writing and directing for M*A*S*H. He directed one episode in his seventh year and wrote and directed two episodes

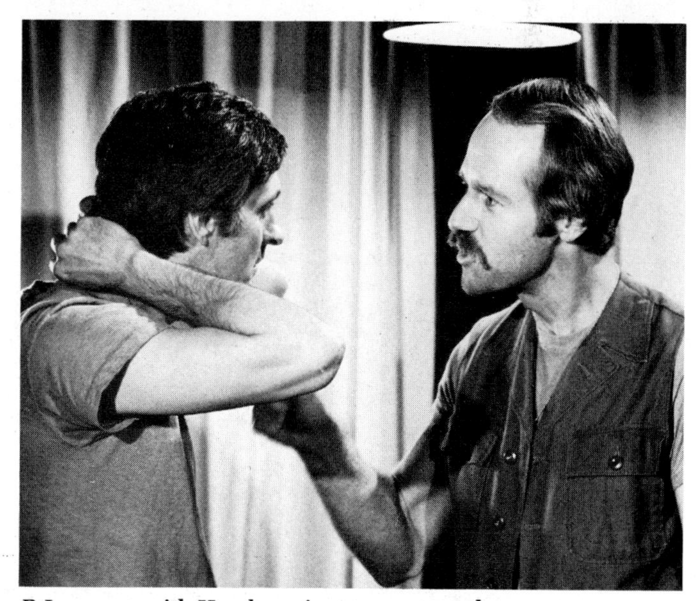

B.J. argues with Hawkeye in a scene over the morality of an unnecessary surgical procedure.

Mike and Alan in a scene with actresses Enid Kent (center) and Mike's wife, Judy Farrell.

Mike and Alan relax between shots with a game of chess.

in the eighth season. It's all made his star rise as far as his industry is concerned, because he is now accepted as a writer/director/actor. Mike finds that each area contributes to the other. His actor's ear for dialogue helps him as a writer. And being on a set as an actor helps the writer in him understand that the success of the script has as much to do with pictures as it does with words.

Mike loves to read, play chess, travel, and write letters. He keeps a correspondence going with many friends, answers most of his fan mail, and fires off letters to newspapers, magazines, and politicians. He mentions that he recently read an article about the death of letter writing, how no one does it anymore, and he thought, "That's really too bad, because I sure have been writing a hell of a lot of them."

Much of Mike's time is taken up with the causes with which he is involved. He constantly receives requests for his help in worthy causes and used to

Mike offers to give Alan and David a karate chop.

say yes to everything but has narrowed his areas of interest down to the situations where he can be most valuable. The issues for which he makes time are what he calls "people issues"—issues that have to do with the quality of life. He's interested in all kinds of "rights"—women's, gay people's, minorities'. He's interested in the issues that make a difference as to whether we will be able to continue to live on this planet—matters like nuclear energy and pesticides. But what he feels is ultimately important is people relating to each other. He supports causes and charities that are on a grass roots level because he doesn't want to front for what he calls "plastic" organizations that say, "We'll make a billion dollars here and we'll give it to the people after we take our cut." The areas that take precedence for him at the moment are the farm workers, the Equal Rights Amendment, prisoners' rights, alternatives to nuclear energy, and children's rights. Mike and his wife Judy (also an actress and writer) are on an advisory board that is developing a show for public television in conjunction with the Educational Film Center and the U.S. Department of Education called "Power House" that deals with the nutritional, mental, and physical welfare of adolescents.

The theme of children always leads Mike back to his favorite cause—his children and his family. He is quick to say, "Way up in front of all this, I should talk about my children and my family and how I enjoy spending time with them. I want to be involved with my kids' lives and I want theirs to be with me. So I involve myself with their school as well as their playtime."

Mike objects to the word "parenting" because he thinks it has come to be something of a "buzz word" and considers the concept too important to dismiss with a word. He says: "I think that being parents is not only an important concept, it's a very massively important part of life." He and Judy take their children and their job of being parents very seriously. They have read all the books, filtered the information through their own feelings and experience, and have come up with a philosophy and a practice that work for them. When the children were babies, the Farrells decided not to leave them with babysitters but to take them with them wherever they went. To this day they often take separate vacations—Judy skis and Mike takes off on his motorcycle—so that one or the other of them is always with the children. This concept has worked some hardships on their own lifestyles and on the lives of some of their friends, and Mike feels they probably overdid it a bit. But he's not sorry.

"Whatever, we ended up with two of the most wonderful children that, in my estimation, have ever walked."

To Mike Farrell, being a parent is the ultimate of everything—the ultimate joy and the ultimate worry. He can't imagine going higher than he's been as a result of his kids—or lower when he's been scared or worried about them. What does he desire most deeply that his kids be when they grow up?

"Happy," he says promptly, "and responsible when it comes to other people."

Mike and Judy have formed a production company, are looking for projects to do, are writing projects of their own, and are getting into business ventures outside of show business, such as opening a natural-foods restaurant and marketing a board game. They are involved and caring people. Mike says, "So we'll be producing and writing and acting and—whatever's out there. The world's a big place and there are a lot of interesting things to do and people to meet and see—so who knows?"

B.J. in a dinner jacket from the "Dreams" episode.

Larry Linville

Larry Linville, as Frank Burns, was the favorite "goat" of both the M*A*S*H unit and TV viewers for five years. There was the time he responded to a cry of "Air raid!," ran screaming from his tent and jumped into a bomb shelter filled with water. His hysteria was barely controlled when he had to undergo a medical examination presided over by a gorilla-suited surgical team. When he discovered that Hot Lips was engaged he went totally berserk, ran out and arrested an ox as a subversive.

Frank Burns has been tripped, tricked, short-sheeted, booby-trapped, flattened, steamrollered, Mickey Finned, and just plain humiliated more often than Tom has clobbered Jerry. As the result of M*A*S*H's popularity, Frank Burns is one of the world's best loved villains.

For five years Frank Burns was the antagonist on the M*A*S*H series—his was the voice of unreason, hypocrisy, and the pettiness we suspect within ourselves, scorn in others, and love to see revealed and triumphed over by Hawkeye and all the others.

Intelligence and high regard for his craft have enabled Larry Linville to shape a character that we so love to see bested, but whom we never hate. We may hate what Frank says, and does, and represents, but never the man himself. He retains a certain tattered dignity and pathos. Though we laugh at his pomposity, he elicits our pity, and we think kindly of his confusion.

Larry Linville is able to walk that kind of dramatic tightrope because he is an experienced, superbly trained actor with extensive background in theater, films, and television.

Larry was born in Ojai, California, on September 29, 1939, but grew up in Sacramento. Always fascinated by airplanes, he decided his future lay in flying jets for the military, so he enrolled at the University of Colorado, majoring in engineering. His interest in acting, begun in high school, slowly took precedence over the engineering and burst into flame while he was at the university in Boulder and

became involved with a theater group called the Nomad Players.

"It was a fine organization," Larry recalls. "The productions were top quality and offered great opportunities for young actors."

Eventually, he made the decision to quit school and work full time with the group, starring in many of their shows. The production he remembers with special fondness was Tennessee Williams' *The Glass Menagerie*.

In 1959 Larry competed for a scholarship to London's Royal Academy of Dramatic Art and won out over 300 other aspirants. During his stay at the academy, from 1959 through 1961, he had several classmates who were also slated for success, including Tom Courtenay, Sarah Miles, Jane Merrow, John Hirt, Ian McShane, and David Warner.

After graduation from the RADA, Larry returned to America and joined the prestigious Association of Producing Artists in New York City, spending a total of eight years in repertory with that group, the Barter Theater in Virginia, and the San Diego Shakespeare Festival. His next move was to Broadway, where he performed with Ingrid Bergman in *More Stately Mansions*. Then he moved cross-country to the Mark Taper Forum in Los Angeles for a production of *The Matter of J. Robert Oppenheimer*. It was in Los Angeles that Larry was discovered by television and made his TV debut in "Judd for the Defense."

"Then I spent three years," laughs Larry, "throwing old ladies down stairs, poisoning Greg Morris, and pounding Darren McGavin in 'Mission: Impossible,' 'Mannix,' 'The F.B.I.,' 'Room 222,' 'Bonanza,' 'Marcus Welby,' 'Here Come the Brides,' and 'The Young Lawyers.'"

Larry's motion picture career has included roles in two highly rated TV Movies of the Week, *Vanished* and *The Night Stalker*, and the feature film *Kotch*.

And how was he led to M*A*S*H and the classic part of Frank Burns?

Larry attributes his good fortune in being asked to audition for the classic role of Frank Burns in the M*A*S*H pilot to a good fairy who pops up from time to time and cracks him over the head with her wand. When Larry arrived for the audition he wasn't even aware of what part he was to read. Metcalfe and Reynolds asked if he had seen the film M*A*S*H, and when he said yes, they asked if he remembered the part of Frank Burns. Larry said yes with enormous excitement, having been impressed with the role and with the actor who played it, Robert Duvall.

Larry was all set to read when the men threw him a curve. There were only seven lines for Frank Burns in the pilot script—not enough to read for an audition. He was therefore asked to read McLean Stevenson's part of Colonel Henry Blake as *though* he were Frank Burns. Larry's training and experience saw him through this difficult task, and he was asked to play Frank Burns.

The next hurdle was CBS's objection to casting Larry, since they had only seen him playing terrifying villains and murderers. Larry says their reaction was, "He can't be funny, he's too frightening, too terrifying. Goodness, you can't have him—he can't be funny." Gene Reynolds and Burt Metcalfe assured CBS that he would *definitely* be funny. CBS capitulated, and Larry Linville was at last approved.

The film M*A*S*H was a phenomenal hit in the late 60s, dearly loved by the public—and almost an immediate cult film. The difficulties of re-creating the characters for a television series were many and serious. Comparisons were inevitable. Twentieth Century–Fox and the series' producers—Gene Reynolds, Larry Gelbart, and associate producer Burt Metcalfe — decided to run the film for the cast just before the pilot was to be shot. The cast decided not to attend, feeling it would be foolish to try to imitate the actors in the picture in any way.

Larry remembers the mood of the cast at that time. "We all pretty much determined, since we were already a rather tight ensemble, that, in effect, to hell with the picture. We'd re-create these personalities with what *we* had to bring to them. I mean, me approximating Robert Duvall who played Frank Burns in the film, is stupid. That is a dumb idea. He does Robert Duvall infinitely better than I do, so the alternative was to reach into my mind and find those things that *I* thought the character should be and, of course, with Gene's and Larry's guidance, create something new."

The pilot of a proposed television series introduces all the characters and settings and establishes

Larry watches cameraman as actor/director Jackie Cooper calls the shots.

the basic premise for the show. The pilot for M*A*S*H had an unusual amount of time for preparation. There were two weeks of just input from various sources—producers, directors, actors—all saying, as Larry tells it, "This would make it better or that might make it better." At the end of two weeks Larry found his original seven lines had grown measurably—as had his importance as a character and his physical "business" on screen.

"Freak things." Larry laughs. "For example, they were supposed to stuff Frank into a duffle bag and throw him out of The Swamp, and that was the end of the scene. The cameras were all set up in the right direction, so, at that point, I offered a suggestion to Gene: 'Let's get the shot with him running outside in the bag.' And Gene said, 'Well, I don't know if that is really necessary, but we'll shoot it.' I got inside the bag and came running out the door down a line of rocks and fell on my can. It was very funny and they cut it into the picture."

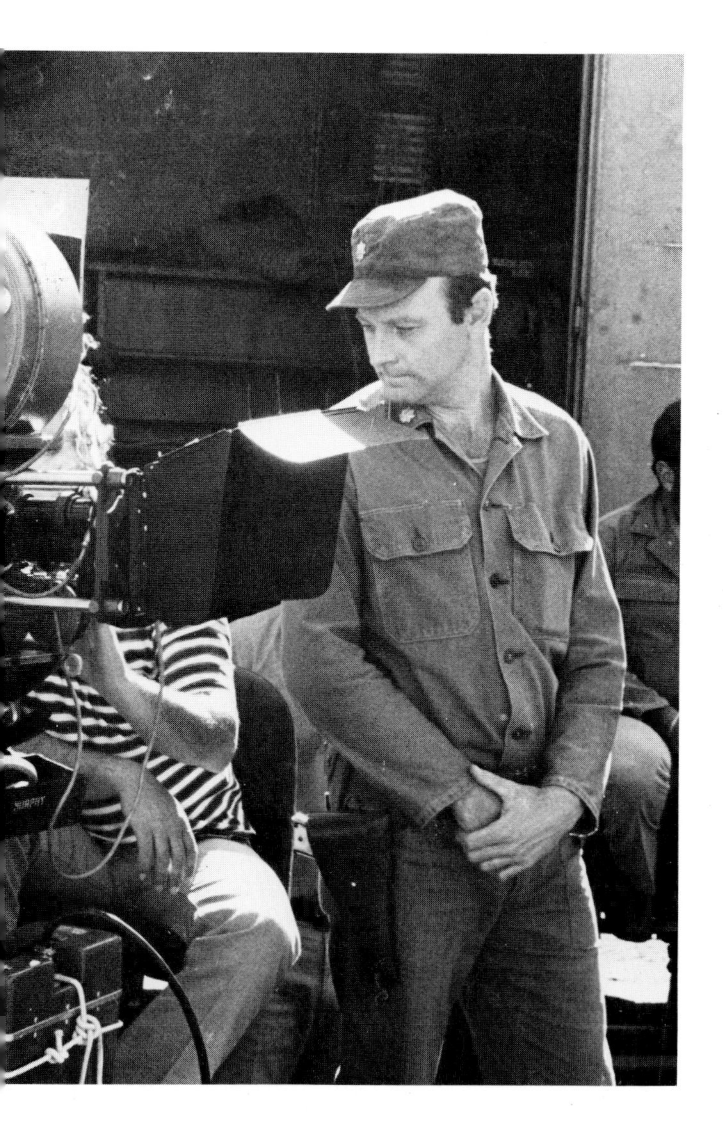

Larry gives the impression that each of the five years he spent on M*A*S*H had a quality peculiarly its own. The first three years were formative ones for the show and the cast. In the first year there was a constant scramble for scripts and directors. The show was in production and scripts had to be rapidly solicited from writers who didn't really know what the characters were like. A great amount of work fell on the shoulders of Larry Gelbart, whose task it was to make the incoming scripts consistent. It was not the fault of the directors or the writers that the network had given the series such a short amount of time to prepare each week's show. Consequently, most of them didn't know what they were supposed to be doing. So, the first year was frustrating—just a constant effort to get the show on track and keep it there. Larry says: "Simultaneous with the frustration was pride, because our efforts were paying off. You could see the results on the screen."

The second year was easier since the writers and directors had watched the show, had seen what was being created, and understood the intention of the creative staff. Larry calls the third year, "Glorious!" and the fourth year "a time to sigh and relax." The fifth year became, for Larry, the period when he felt his own growth potential winding down with the character and a deep, nagging sense telling him the time had come to move on.

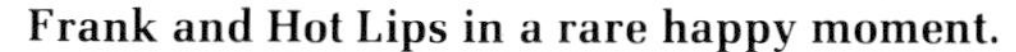

Frank and Hot Lips in a rare happy moment.

Frank in the mess tent with Potter and B.J.

One of the most difficult, delightful, adventurous, and satisfying elements in being an actor is the exploration of the character you are playing and the character's layer-by-layer development. Larry wanted to explore Frank Burns and was assisted heavily by both Gene Reynolds and Larry Gelbart in expanding the character without violating its bounds—that is, it was understood Frank would not suddenly see the light and become a nice guy. Larry recognized that people don't change their basic character, and especially not Frank Burns. The writers could, however, put him into different circumstances and new configurations.

Gelbart often asked Larry, "What would you like to do with your character, and what do you think he would do under those circumstances?"

On one occasion Larry responded with, "Well, I don't know. Frank is so straightlaced. I'd like to see him get absolutely drunk once; totally boiled out."

Gelbart thought that idea was amusing but wondered what Frank Burns would be like if he were thoroughly drunk. Would he be even worse than usual? Larry Linville concluded that Frank would be just the opposite—he would be so sickly nice as to be absolutely repulsive. Gelbart wrote a scene with a drunken Frank Burns that turned out to be

hilarious. Frank came into The Swamp where Hawkeye and Trapper were brewing their horrible martinis and asked for a drink. Looking slightly shocked at this unusual request the men handed Frank a drink, that he promptly drained with nary a flicker.

Larry says: "I was facing the old cliché, which is choke, gag, gasp, sweat, blink. But I have a habit of inverting things and trying to get away from clichés." Larry decided that Frank was a genius drinker and didn't even *know* it. He would take a drink, smack his lips and say something like, "Hmm, tastes like lemonade." This amusing twist allowed Hawkeye to look at Trapper and say, "Must have been the lozenges we put in it." This is a perfect example of why the writers and directors on M*A*S*H look to the cast for creative input from the first reading of a script through completion of shooting.

Larry's favorite moments during his years on the series are not, as might be expected, moments in which he was the central figure. He chortles gleefully over one of those moments when the cast members felt that something had been put over on the network and the TV audience. Gary Burghoff had a scene in which he was running around the compound being shot at, wearing only a towel and his boots. He ran into the men's shower to hide from a spray of bullets and, as the door closed, he dropped his towel. A brief flash of Gary's backside was left in by the editor but cut so quickly and skillfully that nobody caught it. There could be a few viewers out there with particularly good eyesight who are party to a first in television.

Playing Frank Burns for five years was a joy for Larry Linville. His opinion of the moral character of Frank Burns is not complimentary, however:

"I think there is a misconception on the part of a lot of people in this country that Frank Burns is unusual. My hope is that they see he is *not* unusual. He is fairly ordinary. He comes in sleeker packages, God knows. I hope when people think about who they are going to vote for, or who they're going to work for, or whatever, they cast an eye toward Frank Burns and say, 'Now, does this person behave the same way? Am I dealing with this kind of monster?'" Larry continues, intensely and seriously: "Watch for him, be careful of him. There are Frank Burnses everywhere. Learn to know the type. Don't elect them. Don't make them chairman of the board. Frank is a dangerous man because he acts without reason, often without true intelligence, and, perhaps more importantly, with no real knowledge or perception of what consequences an action will bring about. He is not a man with perception and, consequently, he is incredibly dangerous."

What an ominous character to have to play six months out of a year for five years. But there has to be *something* inside an actor to draw on in order to play any character effectively. There has to be *some* of Frank Burns in Larry Linville. Larry thinks there is a definite percentage. He says: "People are always asking my wife, 'Is he really like that?' And she says, 'Oh, hell no!'" But he says that's not totally accurate either, because an actor *must* function out of those things he has inside of him. Larry rummages around and finds parts of himself that could be used for the character. He hopes the things he finds that are like Frank Burns are *small*, but he takes those things and magnifies them—makes them dominant for the five or ten minutes needed when he's acting. He estimates that perhaps five percent of Larry Linville is recessively like Frank Burns. He takes that five percent and makes it 100 percent for a brief period of time. "The British have a wonderful axiom about actors," Larry says. "They say an actor is a self-playing instrument, so you choose those notes that you wish to use for that particular recital and you use them."

The average member of the audience who meets Larry Linville has a peculiar reaction. Larry finds those reactions endlessly amusing. "People are rather odd when they approach me, because there is always a moment of doubt—you know, 'My God, is he really that way?'" When an actor is welcomed into a person's home every week as a guest, the person feels he knows that character. People approach Larry very cautiously, sneaking up on him a bit, wary that he might turn around and "Frank Burns" them. It's amusing to watch their relief and pleasure when he turns out to be pleasant, willing to listen to them, and gratified at their compliments for the show.

Larry reviews a scene with Alan.

Larry's first experience with the popularity of the show and with his own celebrity was a shock. The cast had been working hard during that first season and was dimly aware that the shows were finally running on the air. None of them, however, *felt* any different. Suddenly Larry was aware that people in the streets, in restaurants, were staring. He isn't sure whether he was merely incredibly naive or just too involved and exhausted to understand, but he honestly didn't know why people were staring. He thought, "What the hell are they doing? Why are they staring? Have I dropped spaghetti down my front? What the hell is going on?" He realizes now that it's easy to lose track when you're working so hard, and not know for a while that you're making a huge impression on a great number of people across the country. Larry did wake up, of course, and remembers thinking, "Of course! It's that damned show!" He laughs, and adds, "Since M*A*S*H, I never go into bars."

Larry Linville is not a pretentious, artsy-craftsy kind of actor. He lives quietly in a modest apartment with his wife Vana and 11-year-old daughter Kelly. Why an apartment when he could certainly afford a house in Beverly Hills? Mobility, says Larry. He gets "a little on the tense side" when he's not psychologically and physically mobile. He needs to be able to take off at a moment's notice without having to worry about security or mowing the lawn or the myriad other responsibilities of a large house. He recently took off on the spur of the moment for Texas, where his wife was appearing in a play at actor Earl Holliman's Dinner Theatre.

Instead of using a hot tub or a psychiatrist for eliminating tension, Larry takes his biplane up for a spin. "There's nothing like taking off the end of the Santa Monica airport runway, turning upside down over the ocean and looking at Los Angeles upside down, to put things in perspective," he says. Larry and his wife have built a sailplane, but she has threatened to wring his neck if he tries it out before she returns from out of town. "She's a 5 foot 2, blue-eyed blonde from Texas, and I listen to her very carefully," Larry jokes.

Larry is moving into the production end of the

Frank arrests an ox and a Korean family as subversive spies.

entertainment industry, writing TV pilots and feature films. He enjoys acting, but feels he has created such an indelible impression as Frank Burns that he's finding he's "stuck with it" to a degree. Producers and directors are having difficulty seeing him in any other kind of role. "The public is more adaptable about my changing from Frank Burns than the industry people are," Larry says. When he was in Texas recently, he was mobbed by fans who knew and liked him as actor Larry Linville, not just as Frank Burns from M*A*S*H.

"I'm going to keep working, keep acting," he says, "and hope that the public approves. I'm going to give them their money's worth, their time's worth, and tell them that when they see a red biplane flying upside down through Topanga Canyon—it might be me."

The difficulties Larry is experiencing shedding his Frank Burns character have not soured him in the least on his M*A*S*H experience. He has fond and admiring words for the series and for what it achieved. "M*A*S*H has been successful due to its broad spectrum, its comedic, classic prototypes, the defiance of authority, and the battle against injustice. It sticks pins in hypocrisy as often and rapidly as possible. And hypocrisy was the most valuable element contained in Frank Burns. It was broad spectrum comedy, too. There were some very obtuse lines for PhDs in literature to enjoy, and there were pratfalls for seven-year-olds to enjoy. It was a military comedy, and military comedies were always popular. My hope was that we obtained classic, comedic value, and I think we did. Not all the time, but I think we did here and there. As far as M*A*S*H is concerned, it was a hell of an event and something definitely to be proud of, and something that was quite wonderful to be in."

Harry Morgan

Harry Morgan is Colonel Sherman Potter, the commanding officer of M*A*S*H 4077. Both by Harry's own reckoning and that of the people who work with and love the man, there is little role-playing here. This Morgan/Potter is the actor-surgeon-soldier emeritus for all. He is the c.o. you could trust with your life and what is left of your sanity. He is the consummate performer you find yourself studying, fascinated by the seeming effortlessness of his perfectly honed timing and the comprehension of his craft. In addition, he is the ever compassionate, goofy, empathetic, and entertaining friend to cast and crew, alike.

Asked how he initially felt about the role of Colonel Potter, Harry responds with one word "Ecstatic!" That first reaction has not lessened in Harry's five years on the show; it has only grown. "You know," he elaborates, "in all my working years, I've never been in anything that I have enjoyed more or loved more or been prouder of. It [the part] was as full for me that first moment as it is now. I knew I was getting into a damn good thing."

Harry Morgan is the consummate performer and old pro because his working years stretch back decades, almost to the beginnings of modern American theater in the 1930s. Born in Detroit as Harry Bratsburg on April 10, 1915, Harry attended the University of Chicago with the intention of becoming a lawyer. Somewhere in the public speaking courses of his pre-law studies, though, the joy of making written words come alive for an audience hit him.

The Great Depression was upon the world, and Harry Morgan was selling office equipment in Washington, D.C., with some success but no enthusiasm, when he heard that a new civic theater was about to be established in the city and that *The Front Page* was being cast as the first production. He went around to audition and stayed on for two productions, making a big hit in a small part in the first and in a larger role in the second, *Petrified For-*

est. The professional director hired for these two shows was Day Tuttle who also owned one of the most respected of all the summer stock theaters, The Westchester Playhouse in Mt. Kisco, New York. Tuttle took a liking to Harry and asked him to come to the Playhouse to repeat his role in *Petrified Forest* and stay for the season. Harry, naive about the theater, and unaware of his inordinate good fortune in having a job during those Depression years, left the office-equipment firm and blithely took off for Mt. Kisco in his 1932 Ford. That summer he played the part of Duke Mantee in *Petrified Forest*, appearing with Frances Farmer and Dan Duryea, and also appeared in *The Virginian* with Henry Fonda.

"I just fell into the acting game." Harry laughs. "I didn't know what I was getting myself into and I had no training at all." He thinks of his life as an actor in terms of transitions and this, for him, was the first big one.

After his summer of stock, Harry moved to New York City, sharing an apartment with two other young actors. On Frances Farmer's insistence he went to the offices of the famous Group Theatre where *Golden Boy* was being cast for its Broadway debut. Group Theatre member Elia Kazan, who was then an actor, and playwright Clifford Odets had been to the Westchester Playhouse that summer to look over Frances Farmer prior to casting her in the lead in *Golden Boy*, so, of course, they had seen Harry perform as well. When he walked into the small offices of the theater group for his appointment, Kazan took one look at Harry, snapped his fingers and ran to find Odets. Odets took one look at Harry, glanced at Kazan and said, "Terrific!"—and Harry was cast as the punch-drunk prize fighter in the soon-to-be hit show, *Golden Boy*. The show played to sold-out houses for a year, went to London and then toured the United States. Harry went straight from *Golden Boy* to the Group Theatre production of Irwin Shaw's *The Gentle People* that starred Franchot Tone, Sylvia Sidney, Lee J. Cobb, and Karl Malden, and which ran on Broadway for six months.

Harry says, "In my ignorance, I thought to myself, 'Hey, this acting business is a great life!' Little did I know! Things got rougher from then on. If I had had to struggle at the beginning like most actors, if I had known what I was in for, I'd never have stuck it out. But having such complete success at the beginning, I was stuck with being an actor for life."

Harry remembers one year when he was in three straight Broadway flops and didn't clear a thousand dollars. That year, he and his wife Eileen ate a small can of crab meat and a can of potatoes for Christmas dinner.

Harry says: "When people ask me if their son or daughter should be an actor, I always say, 'No way! If there is *any* way to discourage them, then you should do it.'" He feels saddened by the plight of talented people he has known along the way. "I know people who started out with me who are still hacking away, living truly penurious lives."

There is at least one good memory born of that poverty-stricken period in New York. During one slow period in his career, Harry agreed to be in a playlet, written and directed by Mayor Fiorello LaGuardia, to demonstrate to the Grocer's Association the use of the new food stamp program. Mayor LaGuardia took Harry to dinner, gave him $8 for his services, and a ride home in the official limousine. Harry laughs and says, "Hell, that's the last time I rode in a free limo till sometime last year I think."

Looking toward new horizons, Harry and Eileen took off for Hollywood, where he didn't work for five months. The fates had decreed, however, that it was transition time again for Harry Morgan. David Selznick, for some eccentric reason, was devoting all the enormous facilities and stars of his studio to putting on a season of summer stock in Santa Barbara. One of the productions, *The Devil's Disciple*, starring Cedric Hardwick, was rather short, so director John Houseman (known today for the television series, "The Paper Chase") asked playwright William Saroyan if he had a one-act play that could be used as a curtain raiser. Saroyan said yes and Harry was cast opposite Jennifer Jones in the now classic *Hello Out There*. The play was a tremendous success and a personal triumph for Harry.

Opening night, a gentleman named Charles K. Feldman came backstage to talk to Harry. Feldman explained he was an agent and asked if Harry needed an agent, as he would be pleased to represent him. Harry, again ignorant of the facts of life in Hollywood, said, "Thank you very much, but I *have* an agent," and saw Feldman on his way. Harry's own agent, of the William Morris Agency, had taken no advantage of his client's success and it had made Harry a little angry. He told this story to friend and successful short story writer, John Collier, and mentioned in passing that this nice fellow, Charles Feldman, had been around to see him. John Collier almost jumped out of his skin, then calmed down enough to inform Harry that Charles Feldman just *happened* to be the biggest agent in Hollywood and Harry should immediately march over to see Feldman and tell him he would be *pleased* to be represented by him, thank you very much! Harry followed orders and, as a result, had a contract at Twentieth Century–Fox the next week.

Harry says *that* was the second transition, and though he's liked all the other things he's done in the intervening years—starring on the TV series "December Bride" for five years, starring on "Dragnet" and the "Richard Boone Theatre," doing over 100 films, including such classics as *The Oxbow*

Harry Morgan.

Harry has a serious discussion with Loretta.

Potter reprimands the gang during rehearsal while the sound man sets the proper level.

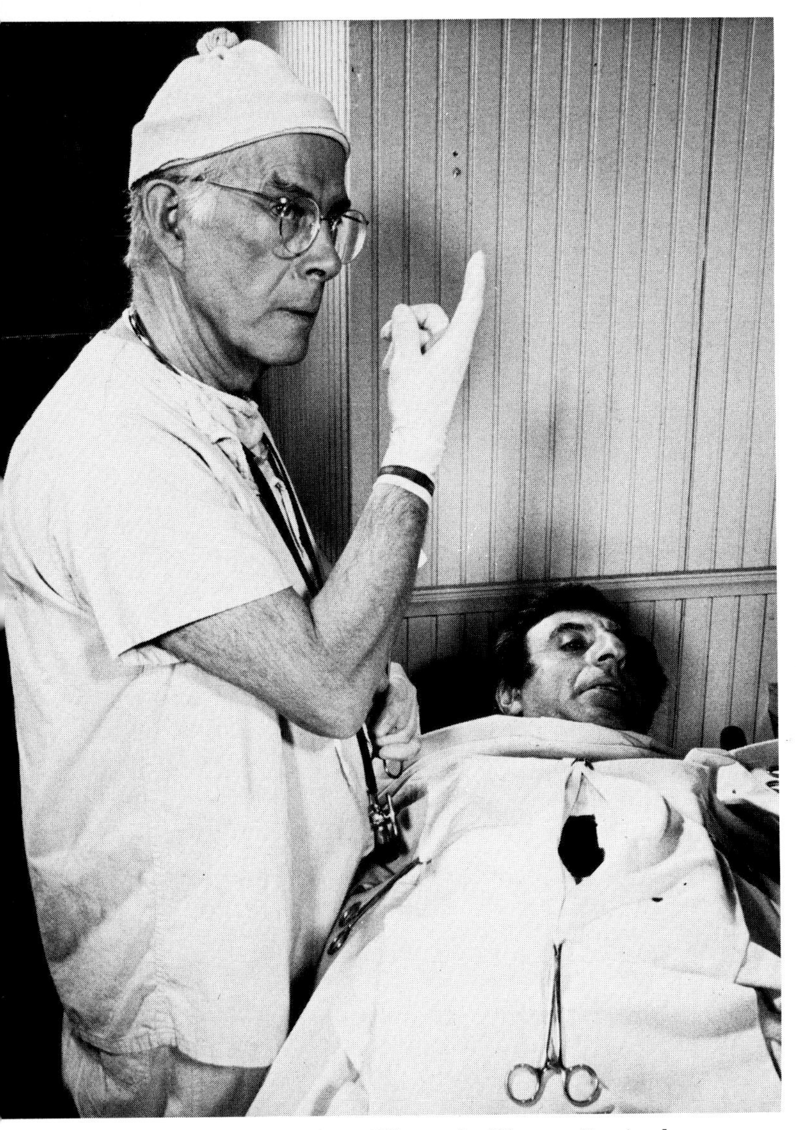

Potter operates on Klinger in "Dreams" episode.

Incident, High Noon, What Price Glory, The Glenn Miller Story, Inherit The Wind, and *Support Your Local Sheriff*—that the *third* transition has been doing M*A*S*H.

"M*A*S*H has meant so much to me professionally, and it's been such a rich, warm experience. There is such genuine sweetness about all the cast. If you met just *one* and had all that sweetness thrown at you, it would be something—but all of them! I know it sounds like I'm trying to throw the bull—but all of them, and Gene [Reynolds] and Burt [Metcalfe]—all of them have that kind of loyal, endearing sweetness."

When McLean Stevenson decided to leave the 4077th, it was clear that the kind if somewhat vague colonel who would rather be fishing would be impossible to duplicate. The new c.o. had to be as different from Henry Blake as possible. Yet, he also had to fit into the manic jigsaw that is the 4077th.

Potter is a regulation, career army man, whereas Blake was a reluctant draftee. Potter ran away from home and saw action in World War I as an underage cavalry volunteer. After the war he earned a medical degree and rejoined the army just in time for World War II. The "police action" in Korea is his third war. Potter is a survivor who has learned that many of the rules of war were written by experience and may just keep you alive. He is a surgeon who, for at least two years before Korea, sat behind an administrative desk, thinking his operating days were over and his retirement was within sight. Yet, here he is, cutting and stitching his third wave of wasted youths. The army can still claim his loyalty, but his tired eyes have long since failed to see the glory of battle.

Harry is impressed with the voice that each member of the cast is encouraged to raise in the filming of the show. "My character is practically me, and that's true, to a great extent, of all the people in the cast," Harry explains. "So, if we get lines that are not honest for the characters we're playing, all we have to do is say so. Sometimes they'll convince you that you're wrong. But if you're not convinced, it will be changed."

The nearest Harry can come in pinning down the person responsible for this atmosphere of liberty is naming Larry Gelbart, whom Harry calls the "creative heart of M*A*S*H."

"I have never met a man who is so courteous 100 percent of the time and so easy—I was going to say, so easy to deal with, but you don't have to 'deal' with Larry Gelbart," says Harry. And it is that ease, that courtesy, that pervades the show and sets it apart from so many others.

As much as Harry loves the pranks on the show he also appreciates the moments of quiet, reflective talk. "I enjoy talking to Loretta, for example, and a lot of that is serious, rather than hilarious. I was going to say man-to-man talk and it is, in a sense, except you're talking to a nice woman. We have a wonderful rapport. If I were to do another television series it would be with Loretta. Can't you find a good series idea for Loretta and me?" he begs.

If the public mostly thinks of Harry Morgan as Sherman Potter, for many, he will always be Jack Webb's sidekick in "Dragnet."

"Listen," he says, "people kid me about 'Dragnet' and that monotone voice we used, but that was terribly difficult to do." Jack Webb, producer and star of "Dragnet," decided that policemen, like doctors, couldn't let themselves become involved emotion-

Harry reacts to Jamie's charm with a Korean child.

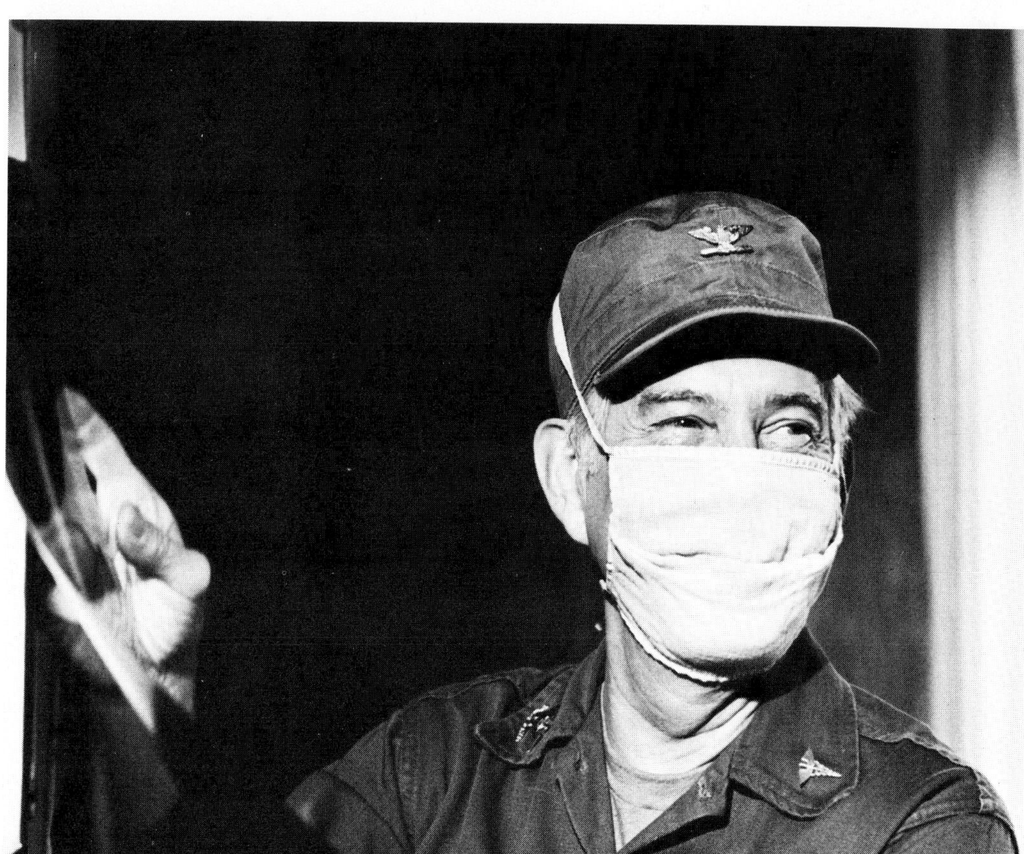

Potter checks an X-ray.

ally with the people they deal with every day because their nerves wouldn't stand up under the strain. He, therefore, invented the now famous flat, monotone voice to indicate the lack of emotional involvement. Harry says, "When, as an actor, you're used to trying to make every line interesting, and then you have to flatten things out like that—that's a damned tough acting job!"

Harry Morgan thinks the best thing about being an actor is the wonderful, lasting friendships formed among members of what he calls "the fraternity." He feels there's a marvelous sense of continuity, that it *all* somehow becomes a big circle. Harry was in *Golden Boy* with actor Lee J. Cobb in the 1930s—coincidentally, Harry Morgan's oldest son married Lee J. Cobb's daughter, Julie. "I still see old friends like Daniel Mann [director of many Broadway and film hits] and [actors] Arthur Kennedy and Ralph Bellamy and Jonathan Winters, and it may be five years between visits, but it's always like it was just last week," he says. "I don't think you find that in other professions. In other professions they just don't work together with the same wonderful intensity and kinship."

Whether Harry retires or not he has a full and busy life with his wife, four sons, five grandsons, and houses in Los Angeles and Santa Rosa. "You think when your children grow up your responsibility is over—but I find that you've just enlarged the circle of responsibility." Each member of the family is usually seen at least once a week and, often, the entire clan crowds in for the weekend. Harry is quite domestic, doing a good bit of the housework and some of the cooking. "I *like* housework and I make a great beef Stroganoff and the best scrambled eggs in the world!"

In the course of his career he has affected peers and public alike. In the words of a fan: "It seems as though he's not acting, he's just talking to you." When asked if there is any higher accolade for an actor and if he really wants to retire and give all that up, Harry Morgan says, "Well, this is a wonderful profession, in the sense that you can keep working until you're 90, *if* you can remember the lines. I may fool around and do a few plays but, after M*A*S*H I may be spoiled—but I wouldn't mind just going out with that blaze of glory. I don't see anything that could follow M*A*S*H."

Potter and his horse Sophie.

Wayne Rogers

There are few roles, in life or in art, more difficult to play than the second lead. Traditionally, he is the guy who doesn't get the girl, doesn't get the medals, and does get the lumps. Ideally, again according to tradition, he should not be quite so clever, handsome, brave, noble, or ultimately victorious as his spotlighted friend.

It is a compliment to the television show called M*A*S*H that Captain John McIntyre, M.D., during his entire four-year tenure, never stood in anyone's shadow. Wayne says of Trapper and Hawkeye, "They shared certain common ends, but got there in different ways." The fact that Trapper, ostensibly the second-lead character, was allowed to share equally those common ends with leader Hawkeye, lent credence and warmth to the whole show. Perhaps that is where the engaging feeling of repertory, of all parts being truly important to the whole, began. And it is that feeling of full development and concern for all characters that has made the 4077th the fascinating family that it is.

Of the character he played with affection and intelligence, Wayne says, "I think he's defined best in relationship to Hawkeye. Hawkeye is a cognitive character—a thinking character. Trapper John was impulsive. Where Hawkeye looks at life seriously and designs his behavior and his actions accordingly in order to reach serious effects, Trapper aimed for the same serious effects and got there in a less straight line. Hawkeye has an element of pessimism in him that said, 'Life is, all around us, not good, and we're here to correct it.' Trapper seemed to say, 'Life as it is is probably not good, and while I know we're here to correct it, let's have some fun along the way. Maybe, just maybe, life can be what we decide to perceive it to be—good or bad.'

"If I were to describe myself," he explains, "I would also be describing what I saw in Trapper John. I am emotionally impulsive and think I have a large thirst for life. I couldn't help but bring those qualities to Trapper's portrait. Luckily, it seemed to

work, balancing off the basic darkness of Hawkeye with a little basic light."

Asked where Trapper and he parted company, Wayne says, "Well, I'm an actor in peace- or relative peace-time and he was a doctor in war. That's a clear separation. I don't think that I'm able to have the same attitude about life and death that Trapper had—that he *had* to have. When you're in a combat situation or you're a doctor, you have to become immune, to some extent, to the constant crisis of life and death. You can go on caring, and Trapper did, but you had better develop some immunity or you're dead. I don't know if I could ever do it. I don't think I'd be quite as brave as those guys appeared to be. Nor could I be as facile or as charming, with the world coming apart around me. But, then, that quality of M*A*S*H is what makes it a show and not a documentary."

All in all, though, Wayne and the M*A*S*H writers drew Trapper John very near to Wayne. So much so that, like everyone else in the cast, Wayne could quickly tell with authority when a line of dialogue did not fit in Trapper's mouth.

Wayne did not start out in life aiming to play Trapper John. Born in the country outside Birmingham, Alabama, he attended Princeton University, majoring in history and graduating in 1954. He joined the U.S. navy and planned on the sea for his future. As a navigator aboard the U.S.S. *Denebola*, a converted Liberty ship, he ran into his first thought of a different direction—acting. While his ship was in drydock at Red Hook, Brooklyn, he had dinner with an old friend who was now a director. After dinner Wayne went to watch a rehearsal of the play his friend was directing and found himself hooked on theater. After nearly three years in the navy, he resigned his commission in 1957 and joined New York's Neighborhood Playhouse. For the next two years he studied acting there with Sandy Meisner, and dance with Martha Graham, finding occasional roles in Off-Broadway productions, including *Chaparrel* with Gene Hackman and Rip Torn. He hustled tables at Schraffts and shared an apartment with two other starving actors, Phil Minor and Peter Falk.

Wayne finally managed to pay the bills with his craft when he landed a running part on the daily serial, "The Edge of Night." In Chicago, he starred in stage productions of *Teahouse of the August Moon* and *Bus Stop*. He went on the road with productions of *Under the Yum Yum Tree*, *No Time for Sergeants*, and *Misalliance*. On a quick trip to Los Angeles one summer, he was cast in a co-starring role with William Bendix in the "Stagecoach West" television series.

Wayne got his first movie role almost in spite of himself. It was in *Odds Against Tomorrow*, directed by Robert Wise. Wise had originally turned him down for the part because he didn't like the actor's photograph. But Wayne's agent persisted, and Wise finally agreed to let him read. After hearing him Wise said, "You've got the part, but I still don't like your picture." Since then, Wayne has appeared in *Cool Hand Luke*, *Chamber of Horrors*, *W.U.S.A.*, *Pocket Money*, and *Once In Paris*, and in several movies for television, including "It's A Wonderful Life" with Marlo Thomas.

The surface personality of Trapper was loved and accepted in the three years that Wayne was on the show, but Wayne felt that nothing much *under* the surface was ever examined. The audience never really found out *why* Trapper felt or behaved the way he did. Wayne says: "You never really knew why he was there, and what it meant to him; where he was going after the war—all of those things were left unsaid."

Asking Wayne why he left M*A*S*H gets a rise out of him. Wayne had never had a signed contract with the studio, and when the time came to put specifics on paper, there were still problems that

Wayne waits off camera.

Jamie, Wayne, and Alan react to something that's gone wrong off camera.

Wayne responds to Alan's wit.

couldn't be resolved. Bill Self, then head of television at Fox, and Perry Lafferty and Bob Wood from CBS all tried to work out the problems and failed. Wayne insists that broken promises were the problem. He says: "I said, 'Wait a minute, you've made certain representations to me. If you're now telling me you're not going to live up to them and that's the bottom line and this is just a negotiation for the purposes of hanging me up, then that's a pass. I'm leaving.'" And he did.

Wayne has one regret about leaving M*A*S*H. He misses the people. He enjoyed them and the good times they had together. "I miss seeing McLean's smiling face and the talks that Alan and I used to have in the morning on the way to location. We *did* have fun on the set. Those people were just terrific."

Asked about his off-camera interests, he says that first and foremost he's interested in reading. He *loves* to read. He *loves* to write. He enjoys the creative process and says you can apply that to all sorts of things other than art—literally to business or politics. "I think problem-solving is an interesting intellectual pursuit. And I am good at solving problems." He enjoys athletics. He plays golf, a little racquetball, and tennis.

Wayne is active in the community. "I think that this society has been pretty good to me, so I try to put a little back in." He is on the executive committees of the Arthritis Foundation and the Easter Seal Society. Wayne has many interests. He would like to act in a play if he could find a good one. And he'd like to spend a couple of years in a university just being a bum—going to the classes he wanted to, not going to the ones he didn't want to. And, no, that wouldn't necessarily have to lead anywhere. It's just the pursuit of general knowledge—as with his reading. He finds an intellectual atmosphere the most calming and satisfying.

He apologizes for not being able to be more specific. "I'm eclectic, and I'm in love with life, so it's difficult to categorize that. So, for me to try to define myself, like, 'Listen, I'm a biochemist whose total life's work has been in the field of x, y, or z'—I can't do that because that just isn't me."

He's a busy, working actor, but Wayne Rogers' serious hobby is finance. He reads the *Wall Street Journal* as faithfully as he does *Variety*. For close friends Peter Falk and James Caan and for himself, he's a skilled, professional business manager, working out of a small office building behind his home in Beverly Hills. It's no toy. It's complete with two secretaries, an accountant, an enormous filing system, and telephones and typewriters that are never quiet. The firm is involved in Canadian forestry, a new microfilm process, condominium development, and other real estate, including a 2,500-acre ranch near Paso Robles, California, that is also the site of a vineyard. The ranch also houses 45 "other people's" thoroughbred horses.

For the most part, Wayne doesn't go to award ceremonies or premieres or big Hollywood functions. He understands, however, that all that is part of the scene. "Somebody once told me," he said, "I shouldn't try to change Hollywood." He flashes that mischievous, quick grin. "That's not my point. I don't want Hollywood to change me."

Wayne and Alan prepare for a scene.

McLean Stevenson

McLean Stevenson is so likable, so easygoing, so completely approachable and natural that it's hard to imagine his having a serious disagreement with anyone. Nevertheless, five years ago he was aggrieved so at what he perceived as untenable circumstances surrounding his work as Lieutenant Colonel Henry Blake on the M*A*S*H television series, that he asked for his release from the show.

He says now, "It was a great experience and a great show, but the war I was having with Twentieth Century–Fox and the war that was going on within me at the time was terrible. Sometimes I think I won the battle and lost the war. Sometimes I think I won the war and lost the battle. I'm not sure. I just know that if I were to make a list of the good and the bad, the good would honestly outweigh the bad. I think the show will go on for as long as the writing remains great and the principal characters wish to stay with it."

More than almost any other fictional character one can think of offhand, it is difficult to know where Lieutenant Colonel Henry Blake of the M*A*S*H 4077 leaves off and actor McLean Stevenson begins—or vice versa. Most of the television public knows a bit about McLean Stevenson's persona from his stints as host and guest on "The Tonight Show" and numerous TV game-show appearances. He *is* Henry Blake—or—Henry Blake is he. Comfortable as an old shoe, familiar as your next-door neighbor—McLean/Henry are "Mr. Everyman." Everybody knows or has known a Henry Blake type—a kind, humorous, easygoing man, in over his head most of the time but trying to make some kind of reason and order out of chaos. The Henry Blakes of the world are happily married and put their children's crayon drawings on their office walls. Henry Blake dreams of being attractive enough to have an affair with a beautiful young woman, but, given the opportunity, 99 out of 100 times he wouldn't or couldn't do it. And if he *did*

do it, he'd probably splash on too much Old Spice after-shave and turn the young woman off because he smelled like her father.

Henry Blake sucked in his pot belly when a pretty girl passed by; let Radar run his command; allowed Hot Lips to intimidate him, Frank Burns irritate him, Klinger amuse him; and gentled Hawkeye and Trapper with his vague, shambling kindness. McLean himself thinks that "I really represented what most young people wished their own dads, or their bosses, or their commanding officers had been like."

McLean Stevenson is neither vague nor shambling. He graduated from Northwestern University and was twice press secretary to his cousin Adlai Stevenson, II, during his presidential campaigns. He was born November 14 in Normal, Illinois, the son of a physician. He graduated from high school there and served as a seaman second class in the navy in the waning days of World War II. A pacifist by nature, he flatly refused to join up and kill anybody. This stance was, at best, difficult for his father, since the good doctor was also head of the local draft board. The result was that McLean was assigned to a para-military unit, the medical corps, where he spent his tour being sick to his stomach. McLean laughs and says, "I really do have a very low gag threshold. Everytime somebody came in sick, if they would barf, I would barf. I couldn't stand the smell of the hospital, and I saw a lot of things that were the result of war that were just awful."

After the service McLean returned to Illinois and attended Northwestern, where he majored in speech, drama, and law. McLean defines himself as "the boy who never knew what he wanted to be when he grew up," so he tried everything—assistant director of athletics at Northwestern; selling medical supplies and insurance; and, as mentioned, selling a presidential candidate. Eventually, he decided to follow his cousin's advice and headed for New York City and a twenty-year acting career leading up to his success on M*A*S*H.

Studying with the best people available can't be anything but an advantage to a young performer, and McLean studied with the top tutors: For acting there was Sandy Meisner; for singing, David Craig, Lehman Engel, and Sue Seaton; and for dance, Hanya Holm and Onna White. McLean did *Brigadoon, Music Man, The Most Happy Fella,* and *West Side Story* in summer stock companies; wrote and performed in revues at the famous Upstairs at the Downstairs cabaret in Manhattan where so many stars got their start; and was in *I'll Always Remember Miss What's Her Name* on Broadway. He also supported himself handsomely as a successful writer of and actor in radio and television commercials for many years.

McLean went to California and immediately popped into the national consciousness as Doris Day's boss on "The Doris Day Show" for two years. He also, simultaneously, did "The Tim Conway Show," filming for Doris Day all day, then taping for Tim Conway in the late afternoon and evening.

With both series off the air, McLean auditioned for a part in "Room 222" that he didn't get. What he did get was a chance to meet "Room 222" producer Gene Reynolds, who shortly afterward called McLean about a part in the upcoming M*A*S*H pilot.

McLean was possibly one of the few people in the world who had *not* seen the M*A*S*H feature film. He promised Gene Reynolds he would go to see it that night, though it was playing in very few locations by that time. He found the movie playing in downtown Los Angeles and went that same night, as promised, settling in just as the lights went down. However, the entire film was done in Spanish with English subtitles. He says, "I did not understand one joke and I hated the movie!"

He went home that night and read the book and went in to speak to Gene Reynolds the next day with a few reservations. He didn't think Henry Blake should be quite the inept bumbler depicted in the film; he felt that the rest of the medical staff should be serious and dedicated instead of buffoons; and he was anxious that the terrible results of war should be shown in a realistic way. He was gratified to learn that Reynolds, writer Larry Gelbart, and the rest of the staff were in complete agreement—and a deal was closed. Or as McLean succinctly puts it, "I took the job, I did the pilot, we were picked up [the series was sold as a result of the pilot], and I did the show for three years."

First impressions are often the ones that are the most accurate. McLean's first impressions of the cast and staff on the first day of rehearsal were astute and remain for the most part unchanged. He remembers sensing that Gene Reynolds was singularly in charge. He still feels that Reynolds is the finest director he has ever worked with and he would walk across the proverbial burning desert to work for him again. He thought Larry Gelbart was a truly brilliant man and Burt Metcalfe was kind, good, and understanding. In Wayne Rogers, McLean perceived a hard-working actor with a great sense of fun and life. They became good friends, and often McLean would turn to Wayne for counsel and advice. "Wayne would always give you an honest answer."

His impression of Loretta Swit has remained the same—that she is one of the few leading ladies and fine actresses who have handled with dignity the difficulties of being young and attractive and vulnerable in the entertainment business. McLean's admiration for Larry Linville is boundless. He considers Larry the most typical within the group of what an actor really is. "A man steeped in acting in the classic sense, skilled, hard-working—a guy with his heels run down and holes in his shoes who still goes on as if, truly, the play is the thing. Larry never changed."

McLean retains the same respect for Gary Burghoff. He still finds it mystifying that Gary and Larry Linville were never nominated for an Emmy Award while he was still with M*A*S*H, yet were, in his view, the two best actors on the show. Alan Alda was something of an enigma to McLean at first, because he found it difficult to believe that *anybody* was no nice, so real, so honest, so kind, and so giving. "I thought of Alan, when I first met him, as somewhere between Groucho Marx and Albert Schweitzer. I still do."

Every member of the M*A*S*H cast has had practical jokes played on him. Is it only because McLean Stevenson is such a funny man, with that wry, self-deprecating sense of humor, that the pranks played on him *seem* so much more hilarious, so much more outrageous and easy to visualize?

McLean still blushes when he remembers an event that he calls "the most embarrassing moment of my life." It happened during the second season on the show. A group of press people had been brought on the set by CBS to do interviews with the cast. McLean was particularly attracted to a lovely woman reporter and was eagerly looking forward to his turn to be interviewed by her. All of the cast members had been given director's chairs with their names printed on them, so the female reporter had

A scene in Henry's office.

seated herself next to McLean's chair in preparation for the interview. McLean had made the mistake of expressing his interest in the lady to members of the cast—and they prepared a trap for him: they had undone the seams that held the canvas chair together. They had also put a "whoopee" cushion (it emits a terrible, loud Bronx cheer when sat upon) on the seat and covered it casually with someone's T-shirt. McLean plopped himself down on the chair and the cushion sounded a loud *bl-a-a-a-t*. As he frantically tried to extricate himself from the chair, the back fell off, the arms fell down, and McLean tumbled from the chair onto the floor. As he lay there mortified, listening to the howls of the cast, the lovely journalist leaned over and said, "That is not only the loudest fart I've ever *heard*, but possibly the most dramatic one I have ever *seen*."

Many people, including those running Twentieth Century–Fox at the time, thought that McLean's request to leave M*A*S*H at the end of his second season was an attempt to generate a higher salary. McLean insists that this was not true. He was, in fact, offered twice his salary if he would come back for the run of his five-year contract. He refused, but did come back for the third year at his original salary but with Fox's agreement to let him leave at the end of that season. His gripe was against what he felt was the total disregard Fox had for the most basic comforts due the M*A*S*H cast and crew.

McLean says: "I could not understand Twentieth Century–Fox. I wasn't demanding anything very odd. I was asking for a place to dress. I was asking for some kind of air to be pumped into the stage to combat the 110-degree heat we endured there during July and August. I was asking that we might have a place to sit when we were on location that wouldn't be 150 degrees inside. [A little tent was finally put up so that the cast could, at least, sit in the shade.] I wasn't asking for a place to park my car, I just wanted a place to go to the bathroom. We

Henry gets walked all over.

had to go all the way to the make-up department to use the bathroom. I couldn't understand why we even had to *ask* for these things."

McLean had been to see Bill Self, then head of Twentieth Century–Fox Television, about these problems. He had been to the M*A*S*H production staff, who would gladly have given the actors air-conditioned trailers and anything else they wanted, but were helpless to combat the disinterest they met at every step from the studio, which was going through a transition and in the process of a redistribution of personnel.

The breaking point for McLean came one cold morning on location in the Santa Monica mountains. There was frost on the ground, and the cast arrived at dawn to discover that there was no heat, no water, and no coffee. McLean blew a fuse, drove down the highway a few miles to a diner and called the studio. He left word with the studio guard to tell Bill Self to call McLean Stevenson at Al's Diner when he arrived for work. Bill Self called him there, and McLean told him he was going to sit there until there was heat and water and coffee, and he didn't give a damn if it cost the studio money or if the show fell behind. McLean says that, with his ire spent, he realized "that I was really dealing with the wrong man. It was now a committee and a computer who ran the studio, and the committee was made up mostly of people who were not even in the business of producing television or motion pictures."

So why did he leave? Because he saw these problems as insurmountable, insufferable, and unresolvable. McLean also admits that he'd been hosting "The Tonight Show" a lot and was tired. He had spent five years playing ensemble roles, and he wanted to do his own thing. "I felt there was a lot more money to be had with a lot less aggravation. And that turned out to be true."

McLean's final show for M*A*S*H, the death of Henry Blake, probably evoked more mail and caused more talk and comment than any TV show in history. McLean had extremely mixed feelings about the decision to have Henry killed in a plane crash on his way home from Korea. Producers Reynolds and Gelbart sprang the ending on the cast at the last moment, and it was a shock to all. Gary Burghoff, as Radar, read the message with the news of Blake's death to the rest of the characters. It was a difficult moment for McLean. "I stayed long enough to hear Gary rehearse it once and shoot it once, then I went back to my dressing room and cried. Not because I died, but because it was all over."

McLean showered and dressed and left his dressing room to attend the end-of-the-season "wrap" party. He walked behind the backdrop that masked Stage 9 and saw that hundreds of people were there—press, executives from CBS and Twentieth Century–Fox, and family friends. He heard no laughter and very little conversation from the large group, and, suddenly, he felt he couldn't face it. He had been saying goodbye all week and he couldn't bear the thought of going through it all again. He turned away, before anyone had caught sight of him, and left the studio. He has never been back.

McLean says: "I think, as time progressed, I went through a series of feelings about the way it ended. . . . From being angry at Larry Gelbart and Gene Reynolds for doing that, and being angry at Twentieth Century–Fox for being a part of it. I felt it was vindictive—that the real motive was to prevent me from doing a show where I might want to continue being Henry Blake, M.D.—which I didn't—to where I am now, which is that it doesn't really make a damn one way or the other. It did make one hell of a show and one that a lot of people won't forget."

McLean now feels he may have overreacted. He says: "You know all those big problems I was having with Twentieth Century–Fox? Well, that was really problems that McLean Stevenson was having. At the time, if Bill Self had come to the set and said, 'Gee, you guys are doing a great job but it's hot in here, let me get you a fan'—I'd probably still be doing the show."

It's obvious that McLean is a much more secure man today, a man more at ease with himself and his place as a performer—and with the ability to differentiate between the two.

McLean loves spending time with his daughter, writing, and playing golf with his friends on public courses. ("Mr. Everyman" feels intimidated by country clubs.) He is longing to direct and has a property he thinks will be accepted by one of the networks, with him as director. He recently was surprised and thrilled when a prominent director came to him with an offer to play a dramatic role in a feature film. "They didn't even want me to read for the part," McLean says; "it was just offered to me." However, he promptly began worrying and wondering whether he had the ability to meet the challenge. He asked if he could learn a scene and do it with the leading lady, to test himself in this serious part. The producer and the director thought he was a little crazy but they agreed. He learned a twelve-page scene, went onto the sound stage, and worked with the actress and the director for three days.

McLean was ecstatic about the result. "I've got to tell you, I was amazed. I mean, I just exceeded my fondest expectation, and I was so far out of myself and into that character that it was unbelievable. Any reservations I had were quickly laid to rest." The film, yet untitled, will be out by Christmas of 1981.

Meanwhile, McLean Stevenson is a busy man. He has his series "Hello Larry," his nightclub act in Vegas, his appearances as host on "The Tonight Show," his golf, his fishing, and his outdoor excursions with his daughter. He also works for the Equal Rights Amendment and the American Library Association. He speaks to small groups of housewives around the country about why the ERA should be passed. For the ALA he sends a personal letter as a reward to children who give up a half hour of television a week in favor of reading a book. He says there are now 200,000 kids participating in the program.

Still, with all McLean Stevenson has going on—if M*A*S*H beckoned, he'd go running. But Lieutenant Colonel Henry Blake is dead in a plane crash, isn't he? Yes, says McLean, but he wants to make a point about how much he loved M*A*S*H and how he still esteems the show and the cast and crew to this day. He says if Burt Metcalfe called him and said, "Listen, we decided that Henry Blake survived the plane crash, and he came to shore with three Japanese fisherman and 50 pounds of kelp in his nose, and he's been living on this island in the Sea of Japan with amnesia. He's been found and taken to Japan and rehabilitated and is now coming back to the M*A*S*H 4077. Would you come back as Henry Blake?" that he would yell "Yes!" and go back.

"I would do it," McLean says. "I have the financial security now, so that I could afford to do it. I couldn't do it when I took the part. I know that's a big statement for me to make, but I don't think in the history of television there will ever be or ever was such *real* entertainment, dramatic comedy—however you want to describe it—as M*A*S*H. There never has been a show like it. NEVER!"

David Ogden Stiers

Charles Emerson Winchester, III, has been trained and been destined from birth to shine, to be superior to other mere mortals. Or so he believes. But his struggles to maintain that superiority amid the hurly-burly, the downright sloppiness of a field hospital make for one of the most amusing and fully realized antagonists in television today.

David Ogden Stiers makes us *feel* the man's agony, his horror of mixing it up with this mish-mash of humanity in the totally undisciplined, unstructured maelstrom of the Korean War. We can feel sorry for him, can sense the human being as a victim of his cultural and environmental conditioning, and never dislike him.

David gives credit to present executive producer Burt Metcalfe for a definition of the Winchester character. Burt had seen several of the Mary Tyler Moore shows where David had appeared as a guest star and in which he gave an inkling of the Winchester to come. Burt described that most difficult kind of performing as "lovably unlovable. An absolutely despicable person who still seems to retain some kind of warmth. You don't despise him so thoroughly that you don't want to see him again. You want to see him show up and find out what he can possibly do that's worse."

Larry Linville, as Major Frank Burns, had been the antagonist on M*A*S*H for five years and had come to feel that his character had no place left to go. He felt his role had become strident and narrow and that the writers couldn't get him out of the hole into which they had written him without destroying the character. Linville left the series, and the writers and producers were faced with the job of creating a new villain—one, it was hoped, who wouldn't become impossibly rigid because of a lack of intelligence or sensitivity. Charles Emerson Winchester, III, was born.

As with most of the casting, the suggestion of David Ogden Stiers for the Winchester role met with nearly instant agreement. David recalls

hearing from his agent, who asked if he would be interested in being a member of the M*A*S*H company. He said, "Well, I'll think about it. [Pause.] Okay, I've thought about it. Yes! Are you kidding? I'd love to."

David was born October 31, 1942, in Peoria, Illinois, but moved to Eugene, Oregon, when he was 15. He was graduated from North Eugene High School in 1960, and promptly began his career on the stage at the highly respected Very Little Theatre in Eugene. If one is very lucky as an aspiring actor, one stumbles into a situation where training-in-performance is possible—where the opportunity to play many kinds of roles, to make mistakes, to grow, to polish, to listen, and to learn, is provided. In 1962 David was offered $200 for three months' work as a member of the California Shakespeare Festival in Santa Clara. He stayed on until 1969, playing King Lear twice; at 22 and 26, Polonius and Richard III respectively. He had major roles in *The Mikado, The Royal Hunt of the Sun, The Caucasian Chalk Circle, An Enemy of the People, Man's A Man,* and *Marat/Sade.* It was an invaluable experience, and Stiers obviously made much of it.

After seven years of repertory David wanted to broaden his horizons and left for New York City and the Juilliard School. Studying for two years in the drama division of that prestigious school, he worked at training his voice for speaking and singing. He developed as a dramatic baritone while still at Juilliard, and he narrated and conducted portions of Saint-Saëns' "The Carnival of Animals" at Lincoln Center and played the Devil in Stravinsky's "L'Histoire du Soldat."

As a result of his talent and excellent training, David's career blossomed and took off in many directions. One wonders how he has crowded so much into one career. On Broadway he created the role of Feldman the Magnificent in the musical *The Magic Show.* He played Buck Mulligan in *Ulysses in Nightgown* with Zero Mostel, and appeared with John Houseman's City Center Acting Company on

Charles braving the cold.

Broadway in *Three Sisters*, *Beggar's Opera*, *Measure for Measure*, and *Scapin*.

He performed with the San Francisco Actors Workshop, The Committee Revue, The America Hurrah Theatre, and The Old Globe Theatre Festival in San Diego, appearing in *Measure for Measure*, *Much Ado About Nothing*, and *The Tempest*.

In motion pictures, he debuted in *Drive, He Said* and continued with *The Cheap Detective*, *Magic*, and a cameo role in *Oh God!*

In television he has starred in the highly acclaimed special "A Circle of Children," was in "Sgt. Matovich vs. the U.S.A.F." and "My Luke and I," and was a regular on the series "Doc." He made extensive appearances on other series, including "Kojak," "Mary Tyler Moore," "Charlie's Angels," and "The Tony Randall Show." He also dubbed the Public Broadcasting System's full-length release of Ingmar Bergman's feature film, *Scenes From a Marriage*.

As a drama instructor, David was artist-in-residence at Santa Clara University, was guest artist at the College of Marin, and taught theater games and improvisation at Harvard University.

David's reaction to M*A*S*H, the TV series, has changed radically. He had been working in the theater for the first five years of the show's life—and had, consequently, never seen it.

"I hated the idea of the TV show M*A*S*H, because I had seen and loved the film. It was only after I started, when the possibility of joining was imminent, that I began screening shows, and I began to realize that I loved it in advance of *anything* I'd seen in the movie. Those two guys in the film were going to be crazy no matter where they were or what condition they were in. They were going to find a way to make mischief. But, the two guys in the TV series were in pain and were made to be crazy because of where they were and the broken people crossing the operating tables. That realization was the first thing that clued me into the possibility, the breadth, of how much a company this group is, and that there was really good work to be pulled out of me if I stayed as open as I could."

David has given much thought to the internal life and motivations of the character Winchester. "Conflicts occur in him when either his taste, intelligence, or surgical abilities are questioned. And I have a feeling that the man really carries a grudge. I

Charles and Radar think of home at Christmas.

Harry, Mike, Loretta, and David react to a prank in "April Fools" episode.

During rehearsal Alan, David, Loretta, and dialogue coach Marty Lowenheim try out an idea.

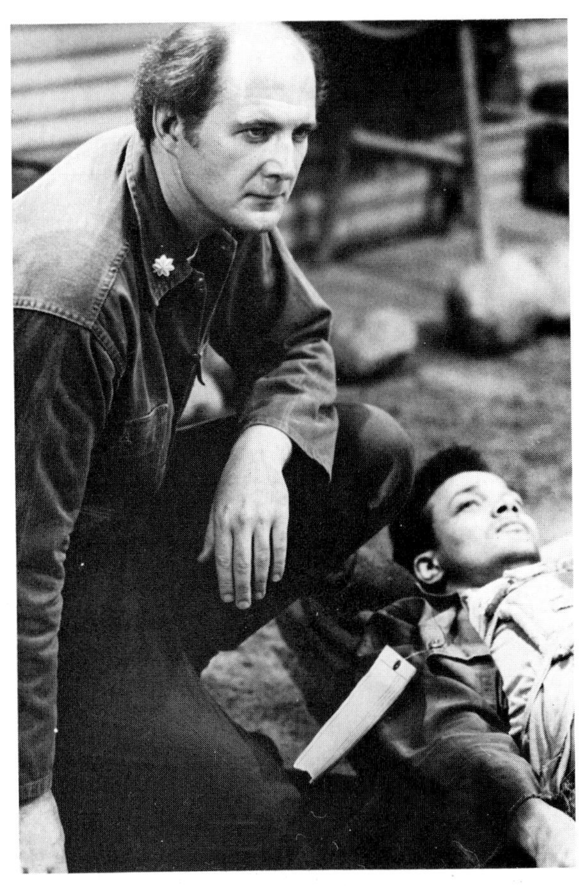

Charles in a triage scene.

Right: David and Loretta between scenes.

think he also defines people and partly judges them by their ability to do or not do—for *him*."

Lately, David thinks the character is softening along perfectly human lines. Winchester's finally beginning to live where he *is* instead of 8,000 miles away, and he's beginning to be able to compromise and put up with working with people whom he, in some cases, detests. "I couldn't be happier," David says, "because it means that I'm going to be able to grow as a character like all people grow. Winchester's beginning to adapt, and whatever form the adaptation takes is incredibly wonderful, fertile, literary ground for the writers and myself to explore and turn over."

Shooting every day, all day, on a series can be taxing—and all actors look for something to keep themselves alert between appearances on camera. Mike Farrell has been known to steal electric carts from the security guards, Alan Alda rides a bicycle (that Mike has also stolen), Jamie Farr skips rope, Bill Christopher reads ancient Greek, Loretta Swit does needlepoint. David Stiers runs over to the recording stage and listens to music being scored as background for films—and he skateboards. He doesn't have much patience for the security guards who get irritated over the behavioral quirks of actors.

"I've been told not to do it. And I often quite cheerfully thumb my nose at them as I'm moving 25 miles an hour on my board. *So sorry!* [Thumbing his nose and sticking out his tongue]."

And, of course, there are the pranks. David came back to work after Thanksgiving and found that someone had had his dressing room repainted. "The colors!—this apoplectic salmon color and snail puce—really unattractive. I turned on the light and, my God, I had retina burn for two hours. It was, I regret to say, an almost luminescent orange." During a day of rehearsal, he said nothing. Finally, he turned to Loretta Swit and said, "Was your room repainted, too?" She perked up and said, "No. Why? Was yours?" (A little too deftly, he thought.) David, all innocence, said, "Yes, and it's *gorgeous*—and colors I would never have picked but that work like gangbusters together. I feel curiously more welcome in it than before. It's really nice." David watched her eyes cloud and, five minutes later, saw her whispering with another actor.

David let it slowly decay over the day. But Mike Farrell could not contain himself. He had to drop by and see this thing that had been done. Regrettably for the pranksters, they had trusted the painter. They had simply asked for orange and purple, but the painter had selected very carefully an orange and purple that would work together. "It's still the wall-covering equivalent of sitting through two back-to-back showings of 'Apocalypse Now,' David says, wincing slightly. "And yet, with soft light on in the room, it becomes almost a rust and the trim burns to almost a brown." Almost.

Stiers' admiration for Harry Morgan verges on reverence and idolatry. He considers Morgan one of the reasons why he decided to be an actor. "Harry is one of the people who pulled me into the business when I was a kid growing up in Illinois." He used to watch Morgan on the "December Bride" TV series and think that if somebody could be that funny, that attractively funny, that consistently, he wanted to do that, too.

"Harry is my professional father," David says. "I laid that on him at the wrap party and he smiled very softly and said, 'Yes, I know.' My own father," David continues, "is a gentle, quiet, loving, very funny man and is as un-theatrical or showbizzy as anyone you'll ever meet. Harry has the same wit, delight, and affection that my father does—but *he's* in show business. And I feel related to him."

David recalls a touching moment when Morgan illustrated for him what he calls "the fullness of being an actor," a kind of completeness of craft. It was during David's first season on the show. On the operating room set, while waiting to recite some lines, Harry was telling David a story about a famous actor with whom he had once worked. Harry continued to tell his anecdote all the way through the director's "Roll camera, please; rolling; speed; marker; *action.*" Whereupon Harry turned around into his close-up position right on time, said his three lines, knew they were correct, and, without waiting for "cut and print," turned back to David and finished telling his tale, with no perceptible shift of gears.

"Harry is what I would love to become," David says. "A person who is at all times fully an actor and fully a person—who considers each a resource of the other and doesn't have to go through an intense plugging and unplugging pattern to get one in touch with the other. It's all continually available and thoroughly mixed."

In summing up his M*A*S*H experience, David is totally affirmative. "No matter how much you read about the M*A*S*H company, the evolution of it, the quite beautiful, human stance it takes, you will not know how much it means to do this work. Re-read everything all the actors have said when interviewed for this book and read very carefully between the lines because their caring is twice as intense as you get from reading it through one time easily. We will all remember that careful cleaving to our own best instincts, and the sharing of the work that *I* expect, logically, not to achieve again."

Loretta Swit

As many as six men have played the primary roles, week after week on M*A*S*H. But there has been only *one* woman. The audience has seen many different versions (and the kaleidoscopic variations thereof) of "men-at-war"—their hopes, dreams, fears, eccentricities, loves, and hates. Those same aspects of "women-at-war" have been manifested for us solely in the character of Margaret "Hot Lips" Houlihan as portrayed brilliantly by Loretta Swit.

Margaret Houlihan—probably the most interesting, multifaceted female character on television today—has been something of a tour de force for actress Loretta Swit. She is everything to everybody—antagonist, protagonist, love interest, archenemy, "goat," friend, ministering angel, comrade-in-arms, daughter, ranking officer, and everything up to and in between. The creative task of discovering this woman and presenting her to us in all her various guises has been a serious labor of love for Loretta Swit over the course of her eight years on M*A*S*H.

Loretta Swit once told a magazine interviewer that one of the great challenges of playing the part of Margaret Houlihan was to keep her humorous, because Margaret is, more often than not, humor*less*. She is, in fact, the butt of the humor on the show. M*A*S*H executive producer Burt Metcalfe read the interview and suggested an idea to the writers for revealing the other side of Margaret. This segment showed Margaret in nursing school, youthful, high-spirited, and fun-loving. An old chum from those school days, visiting the M*A*S*H unit and finding her friend Margaret greatly changed, received this explanation from the character: "There I was one night at a party in Tokyo, and the next morning I woke up in the middle of a war in Korea in charge of a dozen nurses. I figured if I wasn't strong and tough, they would fall apart. I was scared!"

"I find her terribly *human*," Loretta says. "That's

really the most endearing quality Margaret has."

Loretta began her theatrical pursuits by teaching dancing to children. After graduation from high school she made the trek to New York City, studied at the American Academy of Dramatic Arts, and joined Gene Frankel's Repertory Theatre for two years of intensive coaching. She won the job of understudy in *Any Wednesday*, the stage vehicle that launched actress Sandy Dennis; then made her debut in the part opposite Gardner McKay. Like many young actresses, Loretta took to the road, playing one of the Pigeon Sisters in *The Odd Couple*, with a Florida touring company featuring E. G. Marshall and Shelley Berman. Later she toured the country with Celeste Holm in *Mame*.

Loretta arrived in Hollywood in 1969 and became a familiar face immediately, guest-starring on such major television series as "Mannix," "Gunsmoke," "Hawaii Five-O," and "Mission: Impossible." She had been working continuously; thus, when the interview for the Hot Lips role in M*A*S*H came along, she had no inkling that anything momentous was about to happen.

Loretta had just returned from Hawaii and hadn't yet seen the film M*A*S*H, which had become such a phenomenal hit. She was on her way out to go shopping when her agent called to ask if she could meet with M*A*S*H producer Gene Reynolds and associate producer/casting director Burt Metcalfe at Twentieth Century–Fox about the part of Hot Lips Houlihan. Her only thought was, "Well, I'm going to Saks Fifth Avenue anyhow and Fox isn't too far away from there—so, okay."

Since Loretta Swit is the only woman principal of the M*A*S*H series, the development and evolution of her character has been one of the most marked and interesting in recent television history. Any fan of the series knows what the character of Hot Lips was like at the beginning. She was a spit-and-polish, by-the-book, iron-spined warhorse of a major, a martinet to her nurses, and a spoilsport, petty fink, and tattletale to the staff. Secretly, how-

Harry and Loretta sharing a warm moment.

ever, she was locked in a passionate liaison with Major Frank Burns that was to bring her the hated nickname "Hot Lips."

"In my opinion," Loretta says, "Margaret's fallibility and her vulnerability were graphically revealed in the episode called 'The Nurses,' which marked the first major change in her character." In this episode, for the first time, the audience saw the loneliness of Houlihan, how much she cared about her staff, and how painfully alienated she felt because of her rank and position as chief nurse.

Loretta and the creative heads of the series continued to work to develop her character. In the second year of the series, writers Linda Bloodworth and Mary Kay Place conferred with Loretta about her character. "We took her from childhood through boot camp and really felt, when we were finished, that we knew what this lady was all about." The result was the script called "Hot Lips and Empty Arms," which marked the first time the audience was to see Margaret's dissatisfaction with her relationship with Frank Burns, her unhappiness over her stature with the doctors, and her efficiency as a nurse. The character had begun to blossom.

Loretta finally approached Gene Reynolds and Larry Gelbart about ending her affair with Frank Burns. The liaison no longer made the sense it had in the beginning. She asked the creative staff to think about getting her a new beau. They agreed, as did Larry Linville. He felt, too, that Frank Burns and Margaret had exhausted all of the comic possibilities in their funny fights and reconciliations.

Margaret's divorce from her husband, Donald Penobscott, might be considered another major transition, but Loretta and the staff considered it just part of the natural course of events. The audience was to see her try to be happy, to *want* her to be happy and in love; relate to her being afraid of becoming pregnant, yet yearning for children—all

Loretta holding her own in a pillow fight.

Loretta works out a scene with Mike Farrell.

Age 6.

Hot Lips and B.J. react to Hawkeye's claustrophobia.

Right: Hot Lips and Hawkeye speak with chopper pilot.

the wonderful conflicts that make up the heart of Margaret Houlihan.

A milestone for M*A*S*H and for the development of Loretta's character was the series' first "two-parter" [a segment running for two sequential weeks] entitled "Comrades In Arms." Up to that point the conflict between Hawkeye Pierce and Margaret "Hot Lips" Houlihan had been one of the larger threads running through the dramatic skein of the series—one of the major bones in its anatomy.

The two-part episode put Margaret and Hawkeye in a shelled-out house under an artillery barrage—and nature took its course. "It was like the big New York black-out," Loretta laughs. "People turned to each other. In *this* crisis, Margaret and Hawkeye were forced to admit to each other that it wasn't all hate—that there was a lot of affection there, too. It was a wonderful blossoming, a different and intimate look at both characters. The two couldn't take back all that closeness afterward—*she* wanted to, but he wouldn't let her."

Fan mail poured into the studio after "Comrades In Arms," and just the mention of the title of the segment brought a burst of applause at a symposium on M*A*S*H held at UCLA. A note from a student in the audience said that his classmates were all avid M*A*S*H viewers and always com-

mented on the week's show. After the two-parter he explained that the class just stopped its usual work and discussed the show for the entire period. Loretta comments: "It affected them and it affected us. The two characters have been different toward each other ever since."

Somehow, Margaret Houlihan's hated nickname Hot Lips, which was used so often in the early years, has begun to fade into disuse. Loretta feels that the name won't disappear completely, as Margaret continues to be a passionate woman needing to love and be loved. "She's a very giving human being and she's been doing a lot of growing and stretching lately." She hopes the next step will be for Margaret to be allowed to have a new romance with someone who's terrific and strong and *not* a joke. Loretta says, "That would be the next thing I *really* would love—for her to be in love—with all its problems and all its wonderfulness, and see what happens to her then."

Each member of the cast has had memorable, creative moments on the show. Loretta remembers the thrill it was for her to observe the reaction of the cast and crew to her performance in the "The Nurses" segment. In one scene of this segment, Margaret bares her loneliness to a group of nurses who are angry with her—and allows herself to cry and to be human. Loretta describes the moment:

"It was the last scene shown that day at the dailies [the rough, unedited film shot the previous day] and when the lights came back on after the

Hot Lips and Hawkeye during a shelling.

Hot Lips leads the singing in a scene in Potter's office.

screening, everybody just sat there crying, not moving. They ran it again, and when the lights came up the second time they were *still* crying. You can't imagine what that means to an actress."

Each actor has a different reaction to the push-pull of fame and recognition—and lack of privacy—that inevitably occurs for an actor in a hit series. Loretta Swit is an inordinately private person. She likes an orderly existence and works hard to achieve a reasonable amount of grace and graciousness in her life.

Loretta's home in the hills above Los Angeles reflects her spirit perfectly. It is as colorful as a flower garden and balanced beautifully with a variety of wooden surfaces. The house gleams and glows and, for such a perfectly ordered, beautifully chosen menage, doesn't bear even a hint of the chill sterility of having been "decorated."

"My house is an expression of my love for animals and nature," Loretta states. Her home, the place wherein she feels most comfortable, radiates tranquility and order. Watching her function here, it's difficult to imagine that she could be thrown off balance by anything, including celebrity status.

"It's very difficult, there's no question about it," she sighs. "You have to protect what little is left of your privacy as best you can. Your address and your phone number become your best-kept secrets." There are constant demands on her time, and many people who want to talk with her. Over the years she has come to believe that there are a lot worse things than having people tell you how wonderful your show is. "It really is terrific, the love that comes at you from the public. A man once wrote to me from a hospital to tell me how he laughed so hard at an episode that he popped his stitches." But she questions the public's response. Is it she they're responding to, or their idea of who they *think* she is? "You don't want to be somebody's fantasy," she says. "I'm a person who happens to be an actress, and I'd rather not be made into someone I'm not. I love being treated as an equal."

When asked what love means to her, Loretta laughs and says, "Love is the score of zero in tennis. But, seriously, it's the ultimate expression of one's spirit."

Then why hasn't she married? Her direct and honest reason—she doesn't want to be married because she doesn't want children. "People who are in love should be together and should, perhaps, even live together, but for me marriage is only necessary if children are part of the plan. I've found a way of life that I enjoy. If I had a child I would want to give 100 percent to raising that child—and I don't want to give up what I *have* to do that."

Equality and assertiveness were difficult for Loretta in the beginning years of M*A*S*H. She would have liked to be more vocal with ideas and suggestions but was shy. She still considers herself shy, but her confidence in herself has grown enormously. It's still difficult for her to say, "Excuse me, I have an idea," but she does now, and even if there are times when it's not accepted she realizes that the rejection doesn't make her less intelligent or less of a person.

Being a part of M*A*S*H is pure delight for Loretta. "I can think of nothing but moments of mirth, and warmth, and caring for these people," she says. "It's been a long time for me—and for Alan—and we share that at times. We'll be at the ranch [the outdoor setting for the series], for example, and I'll look at him and he'll look at me and we'll say, 'Did you ever think we'd be here eight years later?' We're aware of the history of it, and I think we all feel that we're very lucky to be us. That's an extraordinary thing to say while you're still alive."

Everyone has a best friend, and for Loretta Swit that best friend is Harry Morgan. She beams, "Harry Morgan—there should be one in every home. To know him is to love him, and without Harry the war would really be hell. He holds us together. If you were to make a list of attributes most desirable in a friend and fellow actor—the description would be Harry. He is," she says, "my dear, close friend, my shoulder to weep on—or the one who can turn my tears to laughter. He's just perfect," she concludes, "but then I'm given to understatement." Everyone seems to feel the same warmth for Loretta.

The cast and crew threw Loretta a party in 1975 when she was leaving a few episodes early to take over the lead from Ellen Burstyn in the hit Broad-

Loretta scores a point with the Harlem Globetrotters.

way show *Same Time, Next Year.* "My costumer came up to me and said, 'I must talk to you.' She looked so serious that I became concerned and said, 'What's the matter, what's the matter?' She said, 'Come here,' and led me into the screened-off, operating-room set where everybody was waiting with a wonderful cake that said 'Happy Broadway' on it. It was a wonderful surprise."

The hiatus [the time between seasons] on M*A*S*H is six months long, and Loretta Swit keeps busy during every hiatus every year. Just before beginning the series she made her first feature film, *Stand Up and Be Counted*, starring Jacqueline Bisset, evoking the judgment that her performance was "worthy of an Oscar nomination" from the dean of Los Angeles motion picture critics, Charles Champlin. She has since made two other feature films, *Freebie and the Bean* and *Race With the Devil* with Peter Fonda, and has made seven movies for television. She has recently completed a "Love Tapes," a "Muppet Show," and the "Perry Como Show," and at this writing is appearing in a new Blake Edwards film.

Some of that hiatus time has been spent on her other passion—travel. Loretta has been in every nook and cranny of Europe, because the nooks and crannies—and, yes, the three-star restaurants—are what interest her. She's been to the Far East and Australia, which she didn't want to leave. She crams more living into one six-month hiatus than most of us do in six years.

Loretta calls herself a "passionate cook." She sticks mostly to French and Italian cuisine, and any guest in her home can testify to her expertise, and to her compulsion to make absolutely certain that that guest leaves at least five pounds heavier than when he arrived. Her favorite dish is French, rich, fattening, and luscious: *veau aux naix d'acajou* (veal with cashew nuts). Needlepoint fills her home as the result of hundreds of waiting hours on the set of M*A*S*H. "Other people smoke, eat, read, sleep—I do needlepoint," Loretta laughs. "And the nice thing about it is you can do it and talk to your friends at the same time." She reads everything she can get her hands on, paints, and always has a decorating project in some stage of completion.

Her true passion, however, is the promotion of seven organizations that are concerned with humane behavior. She sits on the board of directors of three of these organizations and supports the others. She also has been chosen 1980 chairperson for the American Humane Society, sponsors a participating athlete in the Special Olympics once each year, and is active in behalf of the Equal Rights Amendment.

"I've done promotional spots for the American Humane Society, which covers not only child abuse but the abuse and neglect of domestic pets and wildlife," she says. Wildlife Way Station, another of her enthusiasms, is a two-hundred-acre ranch run by one woman and a staff that is almost totally dependent on donations. The ranch is a refuge for abused, abandoned wildlife in California as well as those from many other parts of the country. Loretta finds the problem very painful. "People in the world are still killing each other, and we're asking these same people to care about animals, which they continue to regard as an inferior species, when, in point of pure fact, they're simply *another* species."

Her public service and her dedication to animals are reflected in Loretta's daily life and environment. She has a house full of porcelain animals and a number of live animals—mostly dogs. The hills near her home abound with small wildlife, so she keeps water and food out for them all year round.

Loretta Swit is grateful for a fortune that has allowed her to do a variety of pleasurable, profitable, and useful things. Because of her willingness to grow as an actress, her great talent, her gallant attitude toward life and the risks she must take in order to live it well, she has avoided being stereotyped.

"I think of myself as an actress, not a star," she says. "And with that premise I feel I can handle a lot of different roles—and I think people agree with me."

She hopes to grow in the role of Margaret Houlihan in the same way that one grows as a human being.

"I like to practice learning every day, as though I were going to live forever. I like to practice what I learn each day as though I will die tomorrow."

BOSTON

The Producers

Larry discusses an upcoming scene.

Larry Gelbart

"Creative force" is a term applied rather loosely in the entertainment industry, but during the four years of his association with M*A*S*H, Larry Gelbart was the personification of that phrase in its truest sense. Writer, producer, researcher, director, mother hen—he was at the heart of the series and even today remains a minor god to its cast.

Larry Gelbart is an energetic man with a twinkle in his eye, a zest for living, and fond memories of his years as one of the guiding lights of the M*A*S*H series.

"There are those times in your life, if you're lucky, when you're just in the right place doing the right thing at the right time, and that was M*A*S*H for me—beginning with the writing of the pilot which took me two days because it was just so right. It felt good. I knew I was writing something that was going to be a pleasure for me. It gets harder, though, as you go along, because you don't want to repeat yourself. That can make you crazy, especially when you are in your fourth year. It's easy to fall into the trap of repetition."

Larry Gelbart was something of a prodigy and when his family moved from Chicago to Los Angeles he lost no time becoming a professional writer. He was still attending Fairfax High School when he began writing for the Fanny Brice radio show and whipping up material for Danny Thomas. And Barbra Streisand wasn't even born yet!

Larry has said that he "survived" his childhood and went on to "survive" one year and 11 days ("but who's counting?") in the service of his country at the end of World War II—writing for the Armed Forces Radio Network.

From the moment of his release from the service, Larry became a writer, singularly and successfully. He wrote for Danny Thomas and the famous old radio show "Duffy's Tavern" for three years; for Jack Carson, Jack Paar, Joan Davis, and, for four years, Bob Hope.

Larry got his start in television when Bob Hope

transferred his radio show to TV. Larry wrote for television specials, did some of his finest work for the now-classic (Sid) "Caesar's Hour" for two years, and received a Sylvania Award for his "Art Carney Special."

Avoiding all possibility of being stereotyped, he wrote two original screenplays: *The Wrong Box* and *Notorious Landlady.* Then, eclipsing himself, he co-authored with Burt Shevelove, the long-running stage hit *A Funny Thing Happened on the Way to the Forum*, that starred Zero Mostel.

In 1972 Gene Reynolds, producer-director, offered Larry the difficult job of writing a TV series pilot based on the popular screen hit M*A*S*H. Gelbart had been living in London when Gene Reynolds was vacationing there. They had dinner together one evening, and Gene asked whether he would be interested in working on something back in the States. Larry replied that, of course, it would depend on what that something turned out to be. Gene later called from California to approach him about doing the M*A*S*H TV pilot.

The first and only condition Larry made, aside from contractual ones, dealt with the tone of the show. Because the picture had had such enormous popularity, and because America was still involved in the Vietnam war, Gelbart and Reynolds both felt an enormous obligation to stay with the spirit of the film and not convert it into a more or less routine service-gang comedy or a high jinx war.

The next creative decision was concerned with which characters would be retained from the picture. One of the doctors from the film was dropped because it was decided that that many people were not needed to tell the story. Reynolds and Gelbart together worked out a story line in England. Gene went back to America, and Larry stayed on in London to write the actual script for the pilot.

Gelbart subsequently signed on with Reynolds as executive story consultant when the M*A*S*H series went into production and, a year later, became co-producer.

The problem of how much to try to duplicate the film for the series was a dilemma. A few ideas from the film were adapted, but these were used up very quickly and wide research was begun for new ideas.

"We retained the public address system from the film as a production detail," Larry reminisces. "However, I think we invented a good many new things in the first few years." The still in The Swamp (the name for the tent shared by Hawkeye, Trapper, and Frank Burns), in which terrible gin is brewed in a contraption that would have given Rube Goldberg nightmares, was a Larry Gelbart invention. He says that although it is true, historically, that doctors consumed a lot of alcohol during the Korean and Vietnam wars, he felt too much time was spent joking and talking about it. Larry believes that a program has two obligations—to be true to its roots in history, yet be aware of what is happening in the present. Too much is known today about the dangers of alcohol abuse for any writer to ignore it, even though people in the 50s were not as conscious of its perils. Larry suggested, in the third season of the show, that the drinking be played down and, although the men still drank, little was made of it.

New ideas become a paramount concern as soon as a pilot becomes a series. Larry calls it "post-pilot panic." "You're told that you're going to be on the air," he says and laughs, "and then you start to think, 'What the hell are we going to *be* on the air? What have we got to say?'" In retrospect, Gelbart thinks that a good number of the first scripts show—if not fear and panic—a groping and uncertainty about how the show would say what they wanted it to say in entertaining terms. They certainly knew how they felt about the subject matter itself.

Larry discusses an upcoming scene.

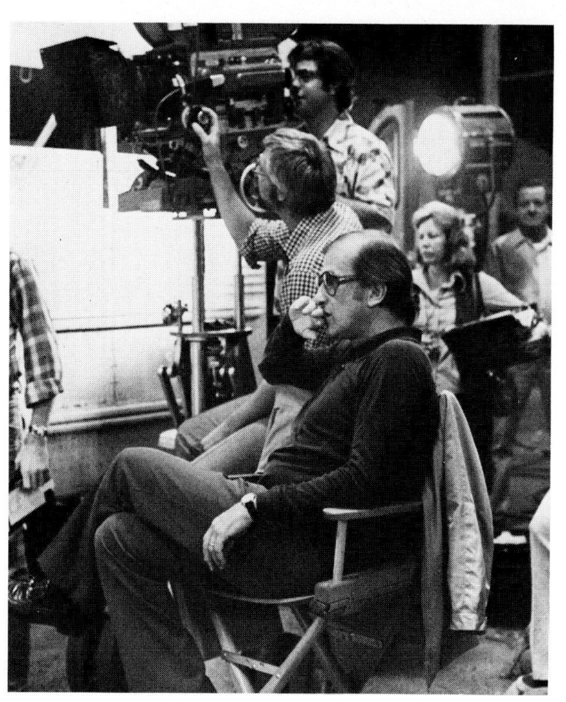

Larry watches a rehearsal of the upcoming scene.

Larry checks camera position for the next shot.

"We were against the war in Vietnam, wars in general, the futility of the doctors, the frustration in healing people only so they could be shot at again, and just the fact that war represents the ultimate breakdown of any kind of sensible relationship between grownups."

Many characters from the feature were added to the cast during the first year. Another surgeon Spearchucker; the Korean houseboy Ho John; and an orderly named Boone were among these, but were discarded as it became awkward and unmanageable to handle so many people on a small screen. The only extra character retained was new—a Gelbart inspiration named Corporal Klinger. Larry says: "Klinger came from *me*, in a word. He was written into one of the early shows, and the idea came to me from remembering that comedian Lenny Bruce, while in the navy, put on a WAVE uniform in an effort to get discharged. It didn't help him any more than it helped Klinger."

Klinger was a character intended for one episode only. But, Larry says, "Jamie, as Klinger, provided a color to the show that nothing else was doing—just an absolute piece of madness every week. He was a lucky accident for us."

Bill Christopher was also not in the M*A*S*H pilot and was the second actor to play the part of Father Mulcahy. The first actor, the one in the pilot, was good, by all accounts, but the staff felt that an actor was needed who was different, who brought certain personal eccentricities to the part. "Bill had those eccentricities," Larry says. "Off camera, he's entertaining and off-beat, and that just slides right onto the screen."

Larry's job, and his primary interest in the first year of the series, was to develop the characters in a new and unique way. The part of Hawkeye Pierce was a delight for him to write because he felt that for the first time in his life he was writing a character he had made feel and sound like what he himself felt and sounded like.

The actors were extraordinarily talented and highly trained, so for Larry Gelbart working with them became like having a finely tuned orchestra for which he could write. He says: "I was constantly, literally, on a bicycle back and forth between my office and the sound stage, orchestrating the script for them," and these fine actors maintained a sense of theater discipline about the words he wrote. The feeling was that the scripts were not there to be improved upon, they were there to be *done*. "That's not to say one couldn't or didn't make suggestions or criticisms. There was that—and we would work from it—but there was none of the rampant practice, as there is in much of TV, of a cast getting a script and just savaging it."

The black-and-white interview show was one of the most unusual segments ever done on M*A*S*H—or any other show. M*A*S*H had come to the end of its fourth season, and Larry had run out of ideas—had gone, as he puts it, "completely dry." Gene Reynolds came to the rescue and suggested simply asking the cast questions, as characters, about what they thought of the war. They asked the cast to respond on tape to a list of prepared questions, had the tapes transcribed, edited the responses, and then shot footage with each of the characters.

Clete Roberts, a newsman with experience in Korea, was an ideal choice to play the journalist who did the interviewing. Roberts asked a few questions on camera that the cast did not expect, resulting in some spontaneous replies. After the footage was edited, the script was written and given to the network for approval—an unheard of and back-to-front procedure in itself.

Larry, reflecting on that experience, calls it "unbelievable." "To me it said, in a way I had never been able to express, that I had finished my work on the show because I couldn't improve upon that. Those were just people talking about an experience, not somebody with a problem at eight o'clock that gets solved at eight twenty-five. It didn't stretch credibilities; these were real people talking about real feelings. It was terribly satisfying. The irony of that show is that it says, 'Written by Larry Gelbart,' whereas, in fact, truthfully it was written by everyone—Roberts and whoever else was there. There are many shows that do not say 'Written by Larry Gelbart,' that are totally written by me, so maybe there is a little TV god who sits somewhere and figures out those credits."

Larry Gelbart left M*A*S*H after four years because he felt himself becoming repetitive. He felt he had done his best work " . . . and my worst, and everything in between." Four years means 97 episodes plus, Larry says, ten scripts that no one ever saw because they weren't up to standard and the staff "ate" them, to use an industry term. He felt he had said it all and didn't want to bore himself or anyone else. Production people on a series spend 13 months a year on the job; they are there at five-thirty or six in the morning and put in a full day's work. It is grueling work and so absorbing that perspective is easily lost. "I once found myself striving so hard

Larry looks at the camera to check its position for the next shot.

for excellence, being so caught up in the work and trying to iron out the bugs in a script," Larry says, "that I suddenly realized I had rewritten a scene that had already been shot."

When pressed to speculate why M*A*S*H has been such a popular show, Gelbart says: "I don't know how to answer that without sounding immodest, so somebody else will have to do it. I'll just say that it was one of the best-written shows on the air to start with."

He stops and laughs at this obvious immodesty. "And it contained one of the best casts anywhere. That's a pretty wonderful combination. It was different; it dared. It still does from time to time. It is a metaphor for life—the camp, the war. The public identifies with it. Not to be all rosy or glowy or sickly sweet, but M*A*S*H is an incredible confluence of a number of talents at the same time and the same place that really results in some superior work."

Burt and Alan on location.

Burt Metcalfe

Burt Metcalfe, the executive producer of M*A*S*H as the series enters its ninth season, began his theatrical life as an actor.

Burt credits the time he spent acting with teaching him much of what he knows about the business of producing for television. "If I were to advise someone on how to achieve what I have, I would tell him to be as varied as possible in his knowledge. I think that if I do well at what I do, it's because I know a little about a lot of things, and much of that comes from acting." However, Burt had quit acting and was a casting director at Universal Television when an old friend and another former actor, producer-director Gene Reynolds, asked him to cast two pilots, one called "Anna and the King," based on *The King and I*, and the other called M*A*S*H, based on the movie. One vanished, the other became history. As an added incentive to lure him into leaving a secure job and taking a flier on a pilot, Burt was given the job of associate producer.

Producing the pilot was considerably more complicated than casting it. "Pilots can be enormously difficult and time-consuming to cast, but everything seemed to fall into place very quickly for us," Burt says. "Gary Burghoff had played Radar in the movie and was available. CBS was already looking for something for McLean Stevenson, and when Alan Alda expressed an interest we zeroed in very, very fast. Loretta Swit and Larry Linville were the images I had in mind for their parts. You know: 'We need a Larry Linville type.' 'Okay, what about Larry Linville?' 'Hey, what a good idea!' It was the same thing later on with Mike Farrell and David Ogden Stiers. They were all the obvious choices, the best people. The only part we had any sort of exhaustive search for was Trapper John. We went through a hundred actors and tested six until Wayne Rogers became the obvious choice from that group."

From the start, Burt explains, the incentive was, in the midst of comedy, to make something of a social statement, to do a truly black comedy with the specter of war ever present. Above all, everyone wished to avoid the traditional, zany "comic doctors show" and inject these doctors with a certain humanity. That they have clearly done what they have set out to do is not, Burt notes, the result of some grand master plan, but simply *that* original intent, laced with a great deal of experimenting.

"In a lot of creative enterprises," he points out, "the revisionists can look back and see all kinds of esthetic significance to having taken this path or that. But when you're in the trenches, so to speak, doing it, you just *do it*. You find yourself in corners and you try to get out of them as best you can, without anything more than your own good instincts and level of taste to carry you."

Associated with the show from the beginning, Burt has gone from casting director and associate producer to co-producer to producer to executive producer.

He remembers being somewhat apprehensive when asked to produce M*A*S*H after Gene Reynolds had gone. "When Gene left to produce 'The Lou Grant Show,' he asked me to go with him. At the same time, I was offered the chance to produce M*A*S*H by myself. I had to make a decision to move out of the comfort of his shadow. There is a comfort in being involved with a man as gifted as Gene, in that you can stay safe in your own little world and not risk the pitfalls that going out on your own automatically presents to you. It was also scary because I had always envisioned that soon after Larry, and certainly Gene, had left, the show would die. I saw an inevitable tag hung on my reputation: 'Oh, yeah, Burt Metcalfe. He was the guy who presided over the demise of M*A*S*H.' I couldn't help thinking I couldn't do it and therefore would be known as the guy it went down in flames with."

Burt sees Gene Reynolds as responsible for getting the show off the ground, shaping it, and pointing it in the direction it was to follow for its duration. "Gene was the catalyst who ignited everything and everyone." He points to the departure of Larry Gelbart as signifying the greatest change in the nature of the show. "The tone of the comedy had to change when Larry left, because we just couldn't equal his comic genius. We were forced to explore other areas, areas that he had not had to bother with, because he was so gifted, so skillful in straight comedy."

It also became clear that if the series were going to be on the air for any great length of time, they could not talk endlessly about war. The war had to remain a specter, of course, but could not be the substance of every episode or, like the years of TV news broadcasts about Vietnam, the impact would be lost in the repetition. The only reservoir of subject matter remaining was the staff of the 4077th. In order to breathe new life into the show, it became necessary to know these people very well and to explore, in depth, what made them tick, what their anxieties were, how they related to one another, how they related to their families back home.

Transitions occurred each time a character was deleted or added. When someone new showed up "they would take you down a whole new path, because you'd have the departure of the old character, the introduction of the new one, and then you'd have to get the new one acclimated and go into everyone's reactions to him," says Burt. The addition of a new character is, of course, an obvious change of chemistry, but Burt also remembers a distinct transition in the overall tone of the series that arose from breaking a television law: in comedy, you can't kill off a character the audience likes. Burt calls that incident a major breakthrough. "The segment was called 'Sometimes You Hear The Bullet.' We introduced a character, a war correspondent who was a friend of Hawkeye's, and we let Hawkeye and the audience care about and learn to like this guy. Then we put him on Hawkeye's operating table and Hawkeye is unable to save him. He dies. Everybody said we couldn't do that. We did and it turned out to be one of the most meaningful shows we've done. It established a pattern that has become more and more familiar. We've capitalized more, over the years, on that mix of comedy and drama that was so clearly hit in that show, to a very worthwhile effect. We are able to weave grim, somber threads into funny things, concurrently."

Burt thinks of himself as a part of a creative team, rather than an august chief executive, although "I have to function as a leader upstairs," he says. [Upstairs refers to the second-floor offices where Burt works with the writing and producing staff.] "Particularly in a season such as we've just gone through, in which you have a complete turnover of the writing staff. Someone has to take hold and say, 'No, we've got to go in this direction now.'"

Burt has written one episode in collaboration with Alan Alda but although he was happy to have a script with his name on it, he nevertheless did not develop a consuming crush on his typewriter. "I feel that I do the other so much better—the guiding and rewriting and polishing and fixing that takes place after you have something on paper. I want to write some day, but to try and write while I'm doing everything else is just too painful. When I wrote that show with Alan ['The Party'], the portion we did together was done sitting in a restaurant with a tape recorder. As for the parts we wrote alone, coming home after a 12-hour day to face that typewriter was overpowering—like a visit to the dentist. That's one of the ways that Alan is so remarkable. He doesn't stop. He has enormous energy. When he'd go home after work or get on the plane to go back east, he'd write as a form of therapy."

Offered a chance to direct an episode in the third season, Burt turned it down. "I was scared," he recalls. "It's inevitable, when you think of the responsibility, to be afraid. When I finally did direct my first show in the fourth season, I was everything the term 'virgin director' implies. It's a very exciting, one-time experience. You're terrified about bringing it in on time, on budget, and on the established mark of quality. But what a satisfaction it was, particularly for a former actor like me. I thought I had given up that particular kind of creative stimulation when I gave up acting and there it was, that same kind of creative rush, that high you get when a take is good and you've had a hand in it."

There is little about the overall show that Burt would change except, perhaps, the laugh track. "It's obtrusive," says Burt. "In American television, the theorists claim it helps rating points, that comedy is contagious, that it enhances one's experience in an isolated living room. I don't believe that and the shows that we've done without it, such as 'The Interview,' were totally successful. And there's no laugh track in the operating room, ever, in any given show."

Burt sees the success of the show as coming from the concept, the writing, and the gifted group of ensemble actors, that have, all together, given us characters that are part of the American scene. The country has taken these people into its homes with affection, appreciating their reality, their dimension, and their honesty.

Burt believes that the public loves not only the characters, but the sensed love that the characters and actors have for one another. He has never ceased to be amazed by the "awe" for the series expressed in the steady river of letters the show receives. He notes: "You don't very often hear people boast with great pride and affection about the fact that they watch M*A*S*H three times a day and 21 times a week, or however many times is possible. That kind of devotion is remarkable. The public is always writing to us about what the show means to them; we hear from wounded veterans in V.A. hospitals, everyone. They tell us we can't imagine how much they appreciate the fact that we are really dealing with war, the horrors, the humanity, the compassion. People demand to know why the rest of television can't learn from us, from the success of M*A*S*H. And I don't know what to tell them. None of us knew that we'd be this successful when we started. There's nobody more surprised by the victory. Isn't there something to learn here? People *will* swallow something other than pablum—swallow it, love it, and demand more."

Burt works on an upcoming scene.

Gene and Alan enjoy a moment together.

Gene Reynolds

One nice thing about the cast, crew, and production staff of the M*A*S*H television series is that they are always anxious to give each other credit. You hear . . . "If it weren't for Alan Alda . . . " or "Larry Gelbart was the genius who . . . " The bottom line is that Gene Reynolds, original producer (and later the executive producer) of M*A*S*H, is the founding father of the pilot and series and is responsible for the quality and high standards set for the show from the beginning.

Gene Reynolds is the man to whom Twentieth Century–Fox entrusted the making of a pilot and series from their most popular feature hit in years. Gene Reynolds went to England and enlisted writer Larry Gelbart to write the pilot, then asked him to continue on with the series. It was Gene Reynolds who talked casting director Burt Metcalfe into leaving his job at Universal—taking a chance that M*A*S*H would become a hit—and then made him the associate producer. It was Gene Reynolds who knew Alan Alda's work, was an Alda fan, and insisted on holding out until the last second in hopes of talking Alda into playing Hawkeye.

Executive producers are not just born, they were *always* something else first—actor, writer, director, and so on. Gene Reynolds was *all* of those things first. As a child he was precocious enough for his mother to put him in an acting class in his hometown of Detroit, although Gene says he would really rather have been out playing baseball. When his father's business crashed, the family moved to Los Angeles and Gene began acting in earnest—as an extra in the *Our Gang* comedies and in *Babes in Toyland* at the Hal Roach Studios.

He studied at the Pasadena Playhouse, meanwhile doing small parts in films, usually portraying the star as a child in flashback sequences. At 14, Gene was put under contract at Metro-Goldwyn-Mayer, where he starred in such films as *Boys Town, Love Finds Andy Hardy*, and *They Shall Have Music* (at the Goldwyn Studios), and others.

During World War II Gene served for four years in the U.S. navy, moving, upon his discharge, to New York City to work in television. He then returned to Hollywood to resume his film career, appearing in *The Country Girl* and *The Bridges at Toko-Ri*.

At this point Gene was discouraged about his acting career. He felt it was going nowhere, he was tired of waiting months between jobs, and he felt it would be better—*healthier*—for him to get up every day and go to a job, any job. He began hounding all the studios for any sort of work. He even took the typing test required of every applicant at a studio. Of this last, he says, "I typed about 11 words a minute, and people were falling off their chairs laughing at my struggles." He tried this avenue for six months before a break came.

Gene was selling suits at a men's store in Beverly Hills and an actor friend of his was working part-time at a store next door. One day the head of talent at NBC-TV came into the store where his friend worked. She said to him, in effect, "What are you doing here?"

His friend cracked back, "You should go next door. Reynolds is selling suits." His friend felt terrible immediately, afraid he had spoken out of turn. But the woman was impressed with Reynolds' industry and called him to ask if he'd be interested in a job in casting. He accepted, of course, and was given the script of "Matinee Theatre" to cast—sink or swim fashion—and his career behind the cameras was off and running.

Gene took a day off from casting to do a one-day acting job for old friend Jackie Cooper on the pilot film of Cooper's series "Hennessy." He was subsequently asked back to direct three segments of the show. When Gene asked for the time off from his casting job to direct these segments, NBC refused—so he quit and took a chance on becoming a full-time director. Gene Reynolds, director, was a success and went on to direct many segments of "The Andy Griffith Show," "Pete and Gladys," "My Three Sons," "Leave It To Beaver," "Hogan's Heroes," and "Peter Gunn."

In 1968 Gene added the producer title to his credits when he produced and directed the pilot "The Ghost and Mrs. Muir" for Twentieth Century–Fox, with whom he was now under contract. In 1969 he began to develop "Room 222" with writer Jim Brooks. The two men did exhaustive research at Los Angeles High School for the series, and Gene began to develop the research techniques that were to pay such dividends in the depth of detail and authenticity seen later in the M*A*S*H series. Reynolds was fired from "Room 222" after the second year, because he and ABC disagreed about whether the show was a comedy or a comedy/drama. Gene considers this firing to be one of his luckiest breaks, since Bill Self of Twentieth Century–Fox then gave him the pilot of M*A*S*H to produce.

Gene Reynolds, Gary Burghoff and Larry Gelbart.

Gene had loved the M*A*S*H movie and the basic format that he describes in this way: "These doctors are in this little cockpit putting people back together again in the middle of a war in this very strange far-off place. It's existentialist in that they had no control about getting there. They didn't volunteer, they were drafted. They can't leave because they are in the army, so that takes the control of their lives away from them, which is an existential position. What they're doing is absurd, it's futile. They're in the middle of a war where everything is designed to destroy, to tear bodies up, to maim, to kill. They're in the business of putting these bodies back together again, only to have them sent back—sort of like recycling people—which becomes like shoving a rock up a hill only to have it roll down

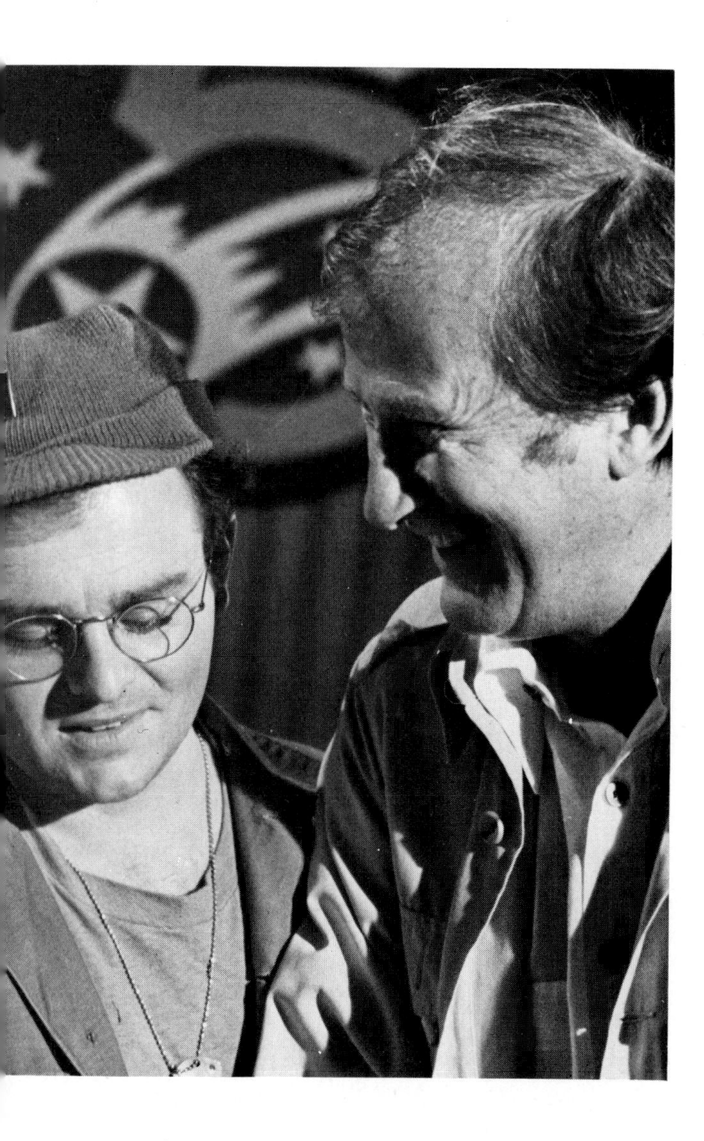

again at the end of the night."

Gene went to England where he hired comedy writer Larry Gelbart to write the pilot. Gelbart remained in England to write, and Reynolds, with casting director/associate producer Burt Metcalfe, began to turn M*A*S*H into the pilot and, later, the series they wanted it to be.

The first person cast was Gary Burghoff as Radar. He had played the part in the film and he was a wonderful actor. The search for Hawkeye and Trapper John was more difficult. Burt Metcalfe went to New York City to look at actors but came up with very little. "It was interesting," Gene says. "It was a very tough category to cast. We needed light comedians and, yet, we needed likely surgeons and attractive, articulate, virile guys. There weren't many of that type around."

The testing of actors turned up Wayne Rogers whom the staff saw as a definite contender for one of the major roles. Then, four weeks before the start date, a major breakthrough occurred. Alan Alda, who had previously refused to commit himself to television, let it be known that he might be interested in doing M*A*S*H. Gene was thrilled, and dispatched a script to Alda on location for a film he was making in Utah called *The Glass House*. Alda was impressed with the script but insisted on a conference with the creators before he would sign a contract. He finished the film in Utah 24 hours before the pilot was to begin shooting, had his conference with Reynolds and Gelbart, was reassured about the seriousness of their intentions for M*A*S*H, and began shooting six hours later.

Loretta Swit and Larry Linville were actors whose work Burt Metcalfe knew and liked, and they were cast as Margaret "Hot Lips" Houlihan and Major Frank Burns without being tested. The part of Father Mulcahy was not cast satisfactorily for the pilot, so Bill Christopher was read and cast for the part between the pilot and the shooting of the first episode for the series. The part of Klinger was created by Larry Gelbart in the second show, and Gene Reynolds thought of Jamie Farr for the part. Gene says: "I had worked with Jamie before and I knew him to be a wonderful comedian, and when this part emerged my only thought was of Jamie. He came in and did it and he has been just spectacular.

"For Colonel Blake I had always had an eye on McLean Stevenson," Gene remembers. He thought McLean was a wonderful, engaging comedian and enormously likable. McLean was interested in doing the series but had thought more in terms of

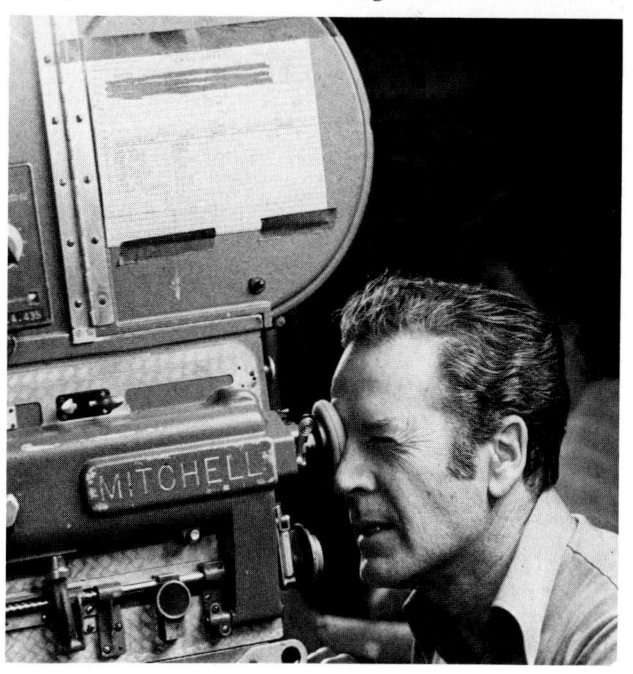

Gene lines up a shot through the camera.

Hawkeye or Trapper. When Gene offered him the part of Colonel Blake, however, he accepted. "I think it was some of the best work Mac ever did," Gene says.

In his present role of creative consultant, Gene continues to advise the production staff on the development of the characters. For instance, occasionally the writers have shown some other aspects of Hot Lips Houlihan—that she is a good nurse and has a soft side—but Gene is cautious about this. In his view, "You can't successfully compromise that authoritarianism too much because you need authority figures in the show. Colonel Blake was too inept to be an authority figure, so it was up to Hot Lips and Frank Burns. They could always threaten to fink on the rest, to call the general if the doctors got out of line. If you throw their characters away, make them too nice, the dramatic tension is gone and everybody's on the same side of the line with nothing in opposition."

Gene Reynolds has three regrets about his time on M*A*S*H. He wishes he could have been around when the sound stage was being assigned to M*A*S*H and gotten a newer and larger stage. He was on vacation when that assignment was made and feels that Fox did not do the right thing by the series when they gave them Stage 9, the oldest and smallest stage on the lot. He regrets that when he was receiving awards for M*A*S*H he never had time to publicly thank all the chopper pilots and doctors and nurses who have helped the show so much. The third regret was that William L. White, author of the book *Back Down the Ridge*, which was Gene's own personal bible in researching M*A*S*H, never knew how invaluable his book was to the show. The book describes the process a wounded man goes through going from an aid station to a M*A*S*H unit, then to Japan. Gene gave it to every new incoming writer and director to study. When he finally wrote a letter of appreciation to the author, it was too late. White had died three months before.

The M*A*S*H series was and is one of the most successful series in the history of television and one of the most well-received critically. Gene Reynolds' determination that the people creating the series must consistently come up with something fresh and different is probably as much responsible for that success as any other factor. He has the same feeling about his new series, "Lou Grant," that is also having phenomenal success. He says: "That's what you have to keep trying for because you can't always do it—you can't *often* do it. But you must try *every* time and then, if you're lucky, you look back at the end of a year and say—'Well, we have three or four shows out of this whole batch that were really unique and successful.'"

In the M*A*S*H feature, the operating room scenes were very explicit; it was a butcher shop. The network executives were worried, as the concept for the television series was being discussed, that going into the operating room would be too shocking for television audiences. Gene was adamant on this point. "They had to go into the operating room!" He felt these men *must* be established as competent doctors so that the buffoonery, the letting-off of steam, was understandable. The brutality of war had to be shown in this way.

The war in Vietnam was going on when M*A*S*H first went on the air, and many people saw the show as an anti-Vietnam statement. Gene admits that the anti-war viewpoint of the show was becoming more and more appropriate as more people began to believe that Vietnam was a dreadful mistake. This coincidence of show and history gave the series more importance than it might have had otherwise.

"It's pretty obvious," Gene says, "that we were talking about a realistic look at war, rather than a romantic one. . . . That if war is soberly looked at, it is not brass bands and ribbons and coming home to your girl. It's innocent young men being slaughtered for the mistakes and sicknesses of older men. Generally speaking, it's a wasteful, dreadful way to settle disagreements and a lot of people suffer, not just soldiers, but civilians on both sides."

At the peak of M*A*S*H's success Gene Reynolds decided to leave the show as creative producer. Why? "Because I thought I had shot my bolt," he chuckles. "I thought I had said what I had to say and I wanted to face a new challenge." He was offered a chance to produce Mary Tyler Moore Productions' "The Lou Grant Show," a new series starring Ed Asner. It was a chance to work with Grant Tinker and a good organization on a show about journalism—a profession Gene feels he might have entered had he not been in the entertainment industry.

"I think you have to risk all," he says reflectively. "You have to start over occasionally. Five years is a long time. People said to me, 'Oh, God, don't *ever* leave M*A*S*H.' But I had the confidence to feel that I wanted to try something else. I wanted to keep going."

Plots and Players

The Compound (on Stage 9)

Alan views film in the moviola over the shoulder of editor Stan Tischler.

Director George Tyne directs a scene in the operating room.

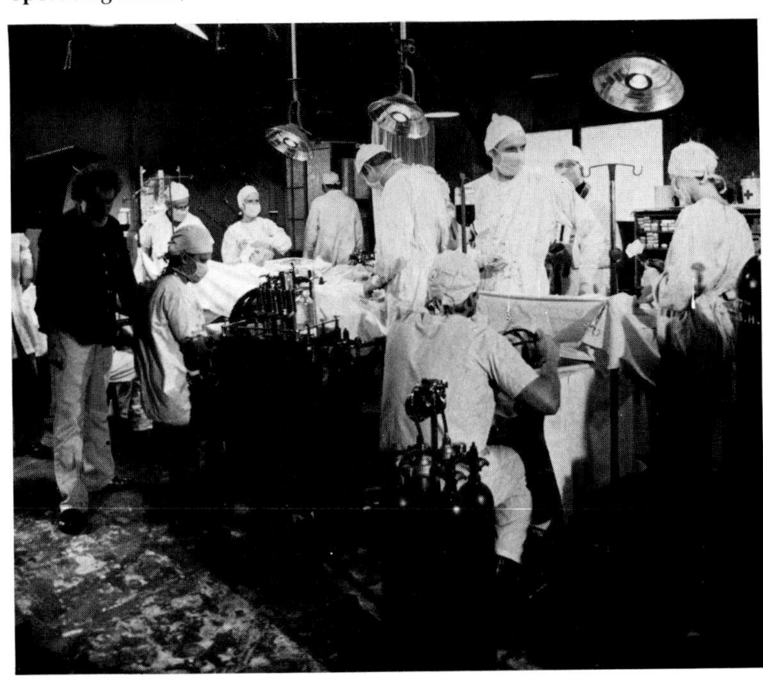

Episode by Episode–the Plots

Eight seasons of M*A*S*H equals 193 hilarious and poignant episodes and 193 crazy plots. Each story line is summarized in the following pages, so you can flip through and do your own instant replay.

* FIRST SEASON 1972–1973 *

Regular Cast: Alan Alda, Gary Burghoff, Larry Linville, Wayne Rogers, McLean Stevenson, Loretta Swit.

All first season shows produced by Gene Reynolds.

M*A*S*H PILOT EPISODE
Young doctors in an Army mobile hospital in Korea alternate saving lives with hours of some notable high jinks.
Guest Cast: Karen Phillip, Timothy Brown, Patrick Adiarte, John Orchard, Linda Meiklejohn, Laura Miller, Odessa Cleveland, G. Wood, George Morgan, B. Kirby, Jr.
Written by: Larry Gelbart
Directed by: Gene Reynolds

HENRY—PLEASE COME HOME
When the 4077th C.O. is transferred to administrative work in Tokyo, Hawkeye and friends launch a wild campaign to get him back.
Guest Cast: G. Wood, John Orchard, Patrick Adiarte, Timothy Brown.
Written by: Laurence Marks
Directed by: William Wiard

TO MARKET, TO MARKET
When black marketeers hijack the hospital's supply of hydrocortisone, Hawkeye and Trapper bamboozle their leader to get it back.
Guest Cast: G. Wood, Robert Ito, Odessa Cleveland, Jack Soo, Beulah Quo, John C. Johnson.
Written by: Burt Styler
Directed by: Michael O'Herlihy

GERM WARFARE
Hawkeye borrows a pint of Frank's blood, then suspects him of hepatitis and works frantically to keep him away from everyone.
Guest Cast: Timothy Brown, Robert Gooden, Patrick Adiarte, Karen Phillip, Byron Chung, Odessa Cleveland.
Written by: Larry Gelbart
Directed by: Terry Becker

THE MOOSE
When a sergeant turns up with a Korean girl he's bought, the young medics spring into action to save her from slavery.
Guest Cast: Timothy Brown, John Orchard, Paul Jenkins, Patrick Adiarte, Linda Meiklejohn, Virginia Lee.
Written by: Laurence Marks
Directed by: Hy Averback

I HATE A MYSTERY
In an epidemic of stealing, Hawkeye becomes the chief suspect, but he elects himself the detective and solves the crimes.
Guest Cast: Timothy Brown, Linda Meiklejohn, Odessa Cleveland, Patrick Adiarte, William Christopher, Bonnie Jones.
Written by: Hal Dresner
Directed by: Hy Averback

CHIEF SURGEON WHO?
When Hawkeye is appointed chief surgeon, Frank complains, and a general comes and declares the place a nut farm and Hawkeye a genius.
Guest Cast: Timothy Brown, Odessa Cleveland, Bob Gooden, Jamie Farr, Linda Meiklejohn, John Orchard, Sorrell Booke, Jack Riley.
Written by: Larry Gelbart
Directed by: E. W. Swackhamer

REQUIEM FOR A LIGHTWEIGHT
Trapper, coached by Hawkeye, enters the inter-camp boxing tournament on a deal to save a beauteous nurse from being transferred.
Guest Cast: John Orchard, Marcia Strassman, Sorrell Booke, William Christopher.
Written by: Bob Klane
Directed by: Hy Averback

COWBOY
When Henry refuses to let a wounded helicopter pilot, Cowboy, go home, things around headquarters begin quite literally popping.
Guest Cast: Billy Green Bush, Alicia Bond, John Orchard, William Christopher, Patrick Adiarte.

Written by: Bob Klane
Directed by: Don Weis

YANKEE DOODLE DOCTOR
When a brigadier general has a film made on the work of M*A*S*H, the surgeons at the 4077 don't like it and make their own film.
Guest Cast: Ed Flanders, Bert Kramer, Herb Voland, Marcia Strassman.
Written by: Laurence Marks
Directed by: Lee Philips

BANANAS, CRACKERS, AND NUTS (AFTER ME, THE DELUGE)
When Hawkeye is denied an R & R pass he feels he needs, he evolves a wild case history for an Army psychiatrist to study.
Guest Cast: Stuart Margolin.
Written by: Burt Styler
Directed by: Bruce Bilson

EDWINA
When a robust nurse is lonely and sad, the other nurses go to some extremes to find a boyfriend for her.
Guest Cast: Arlene Golonka, Linda Meiklejohn, Marcia Strassman.
Written by: Hal Dresner
Directed by: James Sheldon

DEAR DAD
Hawkeye writes to his dad describing Christmas antics, followed by him, dressed as Santa, flying to a battlefield emergency.
Guest Cast: Odessa Cleveland, Jamie Farr, Lizabeth Deen, Bonnie Jones, Gary Van Orman.
Written by: Larry Gelbart
Directed by: Gene Reynolds

LOVE STORY
Radar gets a "Dear John" letter on a record and the doctors try to come to his assistance with a new girl.
Guest Cast: Marcia Strassman, Kelly Jean Peters, Indira Danks, Barbara Brownell, Jerry Harper, Linda Meiklejohn.
Written by: Laurence Marks
Directed by: Earl Bellamy

TUTTLE
Hawkeye and Trapper, with an assist from Radar, make up a fictitious captain in order to donate his salary to an orphanage.
Guest Cast: Herb Voland, William Christopher, Mary-Robin Redd, Dennis Simple, Jim Sikking.
Written by: Bruce Shelly and David Ketchum
Directed by: William Wiard

THE RINGBANGER
Hawkeye, Trapper, and Radar conspire to retire a colonel stateside for his record of too many casualties in battle.
Guest Cast: Leslie Nielsen, Linda Meiklejohn.
Written by: Jerry Mayer
Directed by: Jackie Cooper

Alan often rides around the stage and the studio lot, as he says, "to get a little oxygen."

DEAR DAD . . . AGAIN
Another letter by Hawkeye to Dad tells of camp capers, a correspondence course for Radar, and a cooling between Frank and Hot Lips.
Guest Cast: Odessa Cleveland, Jamie Farr, Alex Henteloff, Laura Miller, Gail Bowman.
Written by: Sheldon Keller and Larry Gelbart
Directed by: Jackie Cooper

SOMETIMES YOU HEAR THE BULLET
Frank throws his back out and applies for a Purple Heart, while Hawkeye weeps for a dead friend and sends an underage boy home.
Guest Cast: James Callahan, Ronny Howard, Lynnette Mettey.
Written by: Carl Kleinschmitt
Directed by: William Wiard

THE LONGJOHN FLAP
During a cold snap, a pair of longjohns sent to Hawkeye becomes more valuable and negotiable than coin of the realm.
Guest Cast: Jamie Farr, Kathleen King.
Written by: Alan Alda
Directed by: William Wiard

MAJOR FRED C. DOBBS
When Frank threatens to leave, Hawkeye and Trapper find it means double duty for them and invent a way to make him stay.
Guest Cast: Harvey J. Goldenberg, Odessa Cleveland.
Written by: Sid Dorfman
Directed by: Don Weis

STICKY WICKET
After a bad session in the O.R., Hawkeye quarrels with Frank over his inadequacies, then finds one of his own patients sinking.
Guest Cast: John Orchard, Lynnette Mettey, Wayne Bryan.
Written by: Laurence Marks and Larry Gelbart
Story by: Richard Baer
Directed by: Don Weis

THE ARMY-NAVY GAME
The 4077th settles down to listen to the Army-Navy game when they're bombarded and left with an unexploded bomb to defuse.
Guest Cast: John Orchard, Jamie Farr, Alan Manson.
Written by: Sid Dorfman
Story by: McLean Stevenson
Directed by: Gene Reynolds

CEASEFIRE
Word of a ceasefire precipitates what proves to be premature plans for abandoning friends, lovers, and the camp itself. . . .
Guest Cast: Herb Voland, Jamie Farr, Patrick Adiarte.
Written By: Laurence Marks and Larry Gelbart
Story by: Larry Gelbart
Directed by: Earl Bellamy

SHOWTIME
While an entertainer does a show from an improvised stage in the M*A*S*H compound, the comedy and drama of the doctors' lives go on.
Guest Cast: John Orchard, Joey Forman, Harvey Goldenberg, Stanley Clay, Sheila Lauritsen, Oksun Kim.
Written by: Robert Klane and Larry Gelbart
Story by: Larry Gelbart
Directed by: Jackie Cooper

* SECOND SEASON 1973–1974 *

Regular Cast: Alan Alda, Gary Burghoff, Larry Linville, Wayne Rogers, McLean Stevenson, Loretta Swit.

All second season shows produced by Gene Reynolds and Larry Gelbart.

DIVIDED WE STAND
Personnel of the 4077th, threatened with reassignment, try to make a good impression on a psychiatrist but soon revert to their wacky ways.
Guest Cast: Anthony Holland.
Written by: Larry Gelbart
Directed by: Jackie Cooper

RADAR'S REPORT
Unrequited love, death, danger, duty, and tomfoolery make up a typical week with the 4077th.
Guest Cast: Joan Van Ark, Alan Arbus, Tom Dever, Derick Shimatsu.
Written by: Laurence Marks
Story by: Sheldon Keller
Directed by: Jackie Cooper

5 O'CLOCK CHARLIE
Daily bombing runs near the hospital by an inept North Korean pilot become the leading spectator sport until Frank spoils the fun.
Written by: Larry Gelbart and Laurence Marks
Story by: Keith Walker
Directed by: Norman Tokar

FOR THE GOOD OF THE OUTFIT
Hawkeye and Trapper are determined to make an issue of the accidental shelling of a South Korean village by U.S. artillery.
Guest Cast: Frank Aletter.
Written by: Jerry Mayer
Directed by: Jackie Cooper

DR. PIERCE AND MR. HYDE
After three days of near-continuous duty, Hawkeye's behavior becomes wackier than usual.
Written by: Alan Alda and Robert Klane
Directed by: Jackie Cooper

L. I. P. (LOCAL INDIGENOUS PERSONNEL)
An enlisted man who wants to marry a Korean girl comes to Hawkeye for help.
Guest Cast: Corinne Camacho, Odessa Cleveland, Jerry Zaks, Burt Young.
Written by: Carl Kleinschmitt
Directed by: William Wiard

KIM
A small Korean boy with minor injuries captures the hearts of all in the 4077th, Trapper's in particular.
Guest Cast: Leslie Evans, Edgar Raymond Miller, Ray Poss, Maggie Roswell, Momo Yashima.
Written by: Marc Mandel, Larry Gelbart, and Laurence Marks
Directed by: William Wiard

THE TRIAL OF HENRY BLAKE
Hot Lips and Frank challenge Henry's fitness to command by reporting some of the activities of the 4077th to the Army brass.
Guest Cast: Hope Summers, Robert F. Simon, Jack Aaron, Bobbie Mitchell, Roy Goldman, Ralph Grosh, Jamie Farr.
Written by: McLean Stevenson, Larry Gelbart, and Laurence Marks
Directed by: Don Weis

DEAR DAD . . . THREE
Hawkeye writes another letter to his dad, telling him some of the wacky goings on in the 4077th hospital unit.
Guest Cast: Mills Watson, Jamie Farr, Odessa Cleveland, William Christopher, Bobbie Mitchell, Kathleen Nughes, Sivi Aberg, Arthur Abelson, Louise Vienna.
Written by: Larry Gelbart and Laurence Marks
Directed by: Don Weis

THE SNIPER
Personnel of the 4077th are besieged by a lone young sniper who believes he's firing on U.S. Headquarters.
Guest Cast: Teri Garr, Marcia Gelman, Dennis Troy.
Written by: Richard M. Powell
Directed by: Jackie Cooper

CARRY ON, HAWKEYE
The flu bug hits 4077th, and Hawkeye is the only doctor left to operate.
Guest Cast: Lynnette Mettey, Gwen Farrell, Marcia Gelman, William Christopher.
Written by: Bernard Dilbert, Larry Gelbart, and Laurence Marks
Story by: Bernard Dilbert
Directed by: Jackie Cooper

THE INCUBATOR
Hawkeye and Trapper battle the brass all the way to the top in their efforts to get an incubator for the unit.
Guest Cast: Robert F. Simon, Logan Ramsey, Vic Tayback, Eldon Quick, Sarah Fankboner, Helen Funai, Jerry Harper, John Alvin, Sheila Lauritsen, Ralph Grosh.
Written by: Larry Gelbart and Laurence Marks
Directed by: Jackie Cooper

DEAL ME OUT
The officers' weekly poker game at the 4077th is interrupted by three separate emergencies.
Guest Cast: Pat Morita, Alan Arbus, Edward Winter, John Ritter, Jamie Farr, Jerry Fujikawa, Tom Dever, Gwen Farrell.
Written by: Larry Gelbart and Laurence Marks
Directed by: Gene Reynolds

HOT LIPS AND EMPTY ARMS
Hot Lips decides that life is passing her by, so she dumps Frank and requests a transfer.
Guest Cast: Odessa Cleveland, Sheila Lauritsen, Kellye Nakahara.
Written by: Linda Bloodworth and Mary Kay Place
Directed by: Jackie Cooper

OFFICERS ONLY
Hawkeye and Trapper save a general's son, and the general rewards the 4077th with an officers' club.
Guest Cast: Robert F. Simon, Robert Weaver, Jamie Farr, Odessa Cleveland, Clyde Kusatsu, Tim Padden, Sheila Lauritsen, Ralph Grosh.
Written by: Ed Jurist
Directed by: Jackie Cooper

THE CHOSAN PEOPLE
A dispossessed family and a girl with a GI baby, all Korean, cause problems for the 4077th.
Guest Cast: Pat Morita, William Christopher, Clare Nono, Dennis Robertson, Jerry Fijikawa, Jay Jay Jue, Bobbie Mitchell.
Written by: Laurence Marks, Sheldon Keller, and Larry Gelbart
Story by: Gerry Renert and Jeff Wilhelm
Directed by: Jackie Cooper

AS YOU WERE
For a few days the 4077th has no casualties; then the front line fighting picks up, and it's back to business as usual.
Guest Cast: Jamie Farr, William Christopher, Patricia Stevens, Bobbie Mitchell, Kellye Nakahara.
Written by: Larry Gelbart and Laurence Marks
Story by: Gene Reynolds
Directed by: Hy Averback

Radar assessing the situation.

CRISIS
Personnel of the 4077th respond in the usual manner when supply lines are cut and they face critical shortages.
Guest Cast: Jamie Farr, William Christopher, Jeff Maxwell, Kellye Nakahara, Alberta Jay.
Written by: Larry Gelbart and Laurence Marks
Directed by: Don Weis

HENRY IN LOVE
While on leave in Tokyo, Henry becomes infatuated with a sweet young thing fresh from the States.
Guest Cast: Katherine Baumann, Odessa Cleveland, Clyde Kusatsu, Sheila Lauritsen, Gwen Farrell.
Written by: Larry Gelbart and Laurence Marks
Directed by: Don Weis

FOR WANT OF A BOOT
Hawkeye is willing to wheel and deal with anyone for anything for a needed new pair of boots.
Guest Cast: Jamie Farr, Michael Lerner, Johnny Haymer, Suzanne Zenor, Sheila Lauritsen, Patricia Stevens.
Written by: Sheldon Keller
Directed by: Don Weis

OPERATION NOSELIFT
Hawkeye and Trapper arrange for an unauthorized but much needed nose job for an enlisted man.
Guest Cast: William Christopher, Stuart Margolin.
Written by: Erik Tarloff
Story by: Paul Richards and Erik Tarloff
Directed by: Hy Averback

GEORGE
Hawkeye and Trapper "persuade" Frank not to request a dishonorable discharge for a wounded homosexual soldier.
Guest Cast: William Christopher, Patricia Stevens, Bobbie Mitchell, Richard Ely, George Simmons.
Written by: John Regier and Gary Markowitz
Directed by: Gene Reynolds

MAIL CALL
When the mail comes, it sets Trapper to planning to desert and Frank to rearranging his stock portfolio on a tip from Hawkeye.
Guest Cast: Jamie Farr, William Christopher, Dennis Troy, Sheila Lauritsen.
Written by: Larry Gelbart and Laurence Marks
Directed by: Alan Alda

A SMATTERING OF INTELLIGENCE
Two secret agents are investigating each other, and the 4077th M*A*S*H makes a hash out of their endeavors.
Guest Cast: Edward Winter, Bill Fletcher.
Written by: Larry Gelbart and Laurence Marks
Directed by: Larry Gelbart

* THIRD SEASON 1974–1975 *

Regular Cast: Alan Alda, Gary Burghoff, Larry Linville, Wayne Rogers, McLean Stevenson, Loretta Swit.

All third season shows produced by Gene Reynolds and Larry Gelbart.

RAINBOW BRIDGE
Hawkeye and Trapper plan R & R, wind up instead with casualties and later the touchy surrender by the Chinese of some U.S. wounded.
Guest Cast: Jamie Farr, William Christopher, Mako, Leland Sun, Bobbie Mitchell, Loudon Wainwright, III.
Written by: Larry Gelbart and Laurence Marks
Directed by: Hy Averback

LIFE WITH FATHER
Mail call brings a hint to Henry that his wife may be straying, and upsetting news to Father Mulcahy, who has a circumcision to preside over.
Guest Cast: William Christopher, Sachiko Penny Lee.
Written by: Everett Greenbaum and Jim Fritzell
Directed by: Hy Averback

SPRINGTIME
It's spring and a grateful patient devotes himself to Hawkeye, while Radar falls in love and Klinger marries by short-wave radio.
Guest Cast: Jamie Farr, William Christopher, Alex Karras, Mary Kay Place, Greg Mabrey, Kellye Nakahara, Gwen Farrell, Pat Stevens, Roy Goldman, Jeff Maxwell.
Written by: Linda Bloodworth and Mary Kay Place
Directed by: Don Weis

IRON GUTS KELLY
When a famed general dies inconveniently at the 4077th, his aide struggles to make it seem that he died heroically in battle.
Guest Cast: James Gregory, Keen Curtis, Bobbie Mitchell, Byron Chung, Alberto Jay, Jeff Maxwell, Dennis Troy.
Written by: Larry Gelbart and Sid Dorfman
Directed by: Don Weis

PAYDAY
Payday brings a windfall to Hawkeye, a bribe to Henry, a pearl necklace to Hot Lips, and a vanished poker pot to Trapper.
Guest Cast: Jamie Farr, William Christopher, Jack Soo, Eldo Quick, Johnny Haymer, Mary Katherine Peters, Bobbie Mitchell, Jeff Maxwell, Leland Sun, George Holloway, George Simmons, Pat Marshall.
Written by: John Regier and Gary Markowitz
Directed by: Hy Averback

The rehearsal table: dialogue coach Marty Lowenheim, writer Dennis Koenig, producer/writer Jim Mulligan (first three at left) sit in on a conference.

O.R.
A bad day in the O.R., with more wounded than the doctors can handle as the war keeps banging away uncomfortably close outside.
Guest Cast: Jamie Farr, William Christopher, Allan Arbus, Odessa Cleveland, Bobbie Cleveland, Bobbie Mitchell, Bobby Herbeck, Orlando Dole, Jeanne Schulherr, Roy Goldman, Leland Sun.
Written by: Larry Gelbart and Laurence Marks
Directed by: Gene Reynolds

OFFICER OF THE DAY
Henry's in Seoul, Frank and Hot Lips are in charge, and Hawkeye is refusing to release a wounded Korean wanted by U.S. Intelligence.
Guest Cast: Jamie Farr, William Christopher, Edward Winter, Dennis Troy, Jeff Maxwell, Jerry Fujikawa, Tad Horino, Richard Lee Sung, Mitchell Sakamoto, Norman Hamano, Mary Katherine Peters, Tom Lawrence.
Written by: Laurence Marks
Directed by: Hy Averback

THE GENERAL FLIPPED AT DAWN
A new area commander, a general, visits the 4077th, scares everyone with his militarism and ends up convincing them he's balmy.
Guest Cast: Harry Morgan, Jamie Farr, William Christopher, Lynnette Mettey, Theodore Wilson, Brad Trumbull, Dennis Erdman.
Written by: Jim Fritzell and Everett Greenbaum
Directed by: Larry Gelbart

THERE IS NOTHING LIKE A NURSE
With the threat of an enemy parachute drop, the nurses are evacuated, and it remains for Hawkeye and Trapper to enliven the camp.
Guest Cast: Jamie Farr, Loudon Wainwright III, William Christopher, Bobbie Mitchell, Molli Benson, Jeanne Schulherr, Leland Sun.
Written by: Larry Gelbart
Directed by: Hy Averback

PRIVATE CHARLES LAMB
Radar purloins a lamb meant for a Greek festival, and Frank is cheated out of an opportunity to persecute a young soldier.
Guest Cast: Ted Eccles, Titos Vandis, Gene Chronopoulos.
Written by: Larry Gelbart and Sid Dorfman
Directed by: Hy Averback

A FULL RICH DAY
Hawkeye tape-records a letter to his dad about a full day in the O.R. featuring a mad Turk, a missing corpse, and a gun-happy officer.
Guest Cast: Jamie Farr, William Watson, Sirri Murad, Curt Lowens, Michael Keller, Kellye Nakahara.
Written by: John D. Hess
Directed by: Gene Reynolds

CHECK-UP
Trapper gets an ulcer and a ticket home until the Army thinks up a new regulation that spoils his going-away party.
Guest Cast: Jamie Farr, Patricia Stevens, Jeff Maxwell.
Written by: Laurence Marks
Directed by: Don Weis

BIG MAC
The 4077th prepares for a visit from General MacArthur, with Frank and Hot Lips very reverent, Trapper and Hawkeye the opposite.
Guest Cast: Jamie Farr, Graham Jarvis, Loudon Wainwright III, Bob Courtleigh, Jeanne Schulherr.
Written by: Laurence Marks
Directed by: Don Weis

ALCOHOLICS UNANIMOUS
Henry's away; and Frank, in charge of the camp, decides that alcohol has become a menace to the 4077th and declares total prohibition.
Guest Cast: Jamie Farr, Bobbie Mitchell, William Christopher.

Written by: Everett Greenbaum and Jim Fritzell
Directed by: Hy Averback

HOUSE ARREST
Hawkeye hits Frank, and Hot Lips sees him do it. It takes a cry of "Rape!" from a lady colonel to change her mind about what she saw.
Guest Cast: Jamie Farr, William Christopher, Mary Wickes, Bobbie Mitchell, Jeff Maxwell, Dennis Troy, Kellye Nakahara.
Written by: Jim Fritzell and Everett Greenbaum
Directed by: Hy Averback

ADAM'S RIB
A GI diet of unending liver and fish prompts Hawkeye to send, with considerable deviousness, to Chicago for an order of ribs.
Guest Cast: Basil Hoffman, Joe Stern, Jeff Maxwell.
Written by: Laurence Marks
Directed by: Gene Reynolds

MAD DOGS AND SERVICEMEN
While a search goes on for a dog that bit Radar, Hawkeye defies Frank to take care of a combat case of hysterical paralysis.
Guest Cast: Michael O'Keefe, Shizuko Hoshi, Arthur Song, Jeff Maxwell, Bobbie Mitchell.
Written by: Linda Bloodworth and Mary Kay Place
Directed by: Hy Averback

THE CONSULTANT
A visiting doctor who's to demonstrate an artery transplant on a critically wounded GI proves, to Hawkeye's dismay, to be a lush.
Guest Cast: William Christopher, Robert Alda, Joseph Maher, Tad Horino.
Written by: Larry Gelbart and Robert Klane
Directed by: Gene Reynolds

WHITE GOLD
When Colonel Flagg turns up wanting penicillin to barter for information, he gets it in the rump—after an appendectomy.
Guest Cast: Jamie Farr, William Christopher, Edward Winter, Hilly Hicks, Stafford Repp, Michael A. Salcido, Danil Torppe.
Written by: Larry Gelbart and Simon Muntner
Directed by: Hy Averback

BOMBED
With bombs falling on the 4077th the work is continuous, and Frank is driven by jealousy of Trapper into proposing to Hot Lips.
Guest Cast: Jamie Farr, William Christopher, Louisa Moritz, Edward Marshall.
Written by: Jim Fritzell and Everett Greenbaum
Directed by: Hy Averback

LOVE AND MARRIAGE
Hawkeye and Trapper help one enlistee to join his pregnant wife and try to stop another from marrying a business girl.
Guest Cast: Soon-Talk Oh, Johnny Haymer, Dennis Dugan, Jerry Fujikawa, Pat Li, Bob Gruber, Jeanne Joe, William Christopher.
Written by: Arthur Julian
Directed by: Lee Philips

AID STATION
Hawkeye and Hot Lips work at an aid station under heavy fire in frightful conditions but emerge with new respect for each other.
Guest Cast: Jamie Farr, William Christopher, Tom Dever.
Written by: Larry Gelbart and Simon Muntner
Directed by: William Jurgenson

BULLETIN BOARD
The bulletin board and the P.A. announcements cue the camp's activities—a lecture, a Shirley Temple movie, a picnic cookout.
Guest Cast: Jamie Farr, William Christopher, Johnny Haymer, Patricia Stevens, Kellye Nakahara.
Written by: Larry Gelbart
Directed by: Alan Alda

ABYSSINIA, HENRY
Henry gets his discharge on points; and while his friends are saying goodbye, Frank concerns himself with taking command. Henry is reported killed as the plane taking him home is shot down in the Sea of Japan.
Guest Cast: Jamie Farr, William Christopher, Kimiko Hiroshige, Virginia Lee, Cherylene Lee, Ray Poss.
Written by: Everett Greenbaum and Jim Fritzell
Directed by: Larry Gelbart

* FOURTH SEASON 1975–1976 *

Regular Cast: Alan Alda, Gary Burghoff, Larry Linville, Mike Farrell, McLean Stevenson, Loretta Swit, Jamie Farr.
All fourth season shows produced by Gene Reynolds and Larry Gelbart.

CHANGE OF COMMAND
Frank settles in as commanding officer, only to have a new one appointed over his head, one that to his chagrin fits in very well.
Written by: Jim Fritzell and Everett Greenbaum
Directed by: Gene Reynolds

IT HAPPENED ONE NIGHT
A freezing night, a barrage that's coming too close, a patient going downhill, and Frank's searching Hot Lips'

tent for his letters.
Guest Cast: Christopher Allport, Darren O'Connor.
Written by: Larry Gelbart and Simon Muntner
Story by: Gene Reynolds
Directed by: Gene Reynolds

OF MOOSE AND MEN
Hawkeye tangles with a tough Army colonel, B.J. helps a GI who's gotten a "Dear John," and Frank looks endlessly for Korean saboteurs.
Guest Cast: Tim O'Conner, Johnny Haymer.
Written by: Jay Folb
Directed by: John Erman

WELCOME TO KOREA
Hour-long episode: Frank's dream is realized—he's in charge, but Hawkeye is unchanged—he skips camp, runs a blockade to find Trapper, who's gone, and welcomes a new surgeon, B.J. Hunnicutt.
Guest Cast: Robert A. Karnes, Arthur Song, Shirlee Kong.
Written by: Everett Greenbaum, Jim Fritzell, and Larry Gelbart.
Directed by: Gene Reynolds

DEAR MILDRED
While Potter writes home, Frank and Hot Lips have a wood carving made for him and Radar rescues a horse and makes him a present of it.
Written by: Everett Greenbaum and Jim Fritzell
Directed by: Alan Alda

THE LATE CAPTAIN PIERCE
When Hawkeye's parents are notified that he's dead, he finds it's no easy matter either to get word to them or to establish that he's alive.
Guest Cast: Richard Masur, Eldon Quick.
Written by: Glen Charles and Les Charles
Directed by: Alan Alda

SMILIN' JACK
The 4077th turns up a sick helicopter pilot who doesn't want to quit and a twice-wounded GI who does.
Guest Cast: Robert Hogan, Dennis Kort.
Written by: Larry Gelbart and Simon Muntner
Directed by: Charles S. Dubin

DEAR PEGGY
B.J. writes home to his wife, reporting Klinger's escape attempts, the visit of a formidable chaplain, and one of Frank's goof-ups.
Guest Cast: William Christopher, Ned Beatty, Dennis Troy.
Written by: Jim Fritzell and Everett Greenbaum
Directed by: Burt Metcalfe

HEY, DOC
Quid pro quo at the 4077th: two bottles of Scotch for secret surgery, a tank to scare off snipers for an unauthorized shot of penicillin.
Guest Cast: William Christopher, Frank Marth, Bruce Kirby, Ted Hamilton.
Written by: Rich Mittleman
Directed by: William Jurgensen

THE KIDS
The 4077th plays host to kids bombed out of their orphanage, and at the same time has to deliver a baby and care for battle casualties.
Guest Cast: William Christopher, Ann Doran, Mitchell Sakamoto, Haunani Minn.
Written by: Jim Fritzell and Everett Greenbaum
Directed by: Alan Alda

THE BUS
Radar, driving Hawkeye and others back from a medical meeting, gets lost and stalls the bus, but all are saved by a surrendering Korean.
Guest Cast: Soon-Teck On.
Written by: John D. Hess
Directed by: Gene Reynolds

QUO VADIS, CAPTAIN CHANDLER?
Intelligence officer and psychiatrist grapple for the fate of a wounded officer who says he's Jesus Christ.
Guest Cast: William Christopher, Allan Arbus, Edward Winter, Alan Fudge.
Written by: Burt Prelutsky
Directed by: Larry Gelbart

SOLDIER OF THE MONTH
Frank has a fever and makes a will leaving all his money to his wife and all his clothes to Hot Lips.
Guest Cast: William Christopher, Johnny Haymer, Jeff Maxwell.
Written by: Linda Bloodworth
Directed by: Gene Reynolds

DEAR MA
Radar writes home to his mother, as Hawkeye conducts the camp foot inspection and Colonel Potter gets some shrapnel in his backside.
Guest Cast: William Christopher, Redmond Gleeson, Byron Chung, John Fujioka, Rollin Moriyama.
Written by: Everett Greenbaum and Jim Fritzell
Directed by: Alan Alda

DELUGE
A sudden deluge of wounded at the 4077th is followed by a fire and a rainstorm to make matters difficult for the staff.
Guest Cast: William Christopher.
Written by: Larry Gelbart and Simon Muntner
Directed by: William Jurgensen

THE GUN
A wounded colonel's gun, a showpiece, disappears, and Hawkeye and B.J. play a hunch and bluff Frank, who has it, into returning it.
Written by: Larry Gelbart and Gene Reynolds
Directed by: Burt Metcalfe

MAIL CALL AGAIN
Mail brings a letter to Frank saying his wife is divorcing

him, and one to Potter telling him he's going to be a grandfather.
Guest Cast: William Christopher.
Written by: Jim Fritzell and Everett Greenbaum
Directed by: George Tyne

THE PRICE OF TOMATO JUICE
Radar gets the help of Hawkeye and B.J. to procure something Colonel Potter says he's fond of but that's hard to come by—tomato juice.
Guest Cast: William Christopher, James Jeter.
Written by: Larry Gelbart and Gene Reynolds
Directed by: Gene Reynolds

HAWKEYE
Hawkeye is injured in a jeep accident and, aware he has a concussion, babbles to a Korean family to keep himself awake.
Guest Cast: Philip Ahn, Shizuko Hoshi, June Kim, Susan Sakimoto.
Written by: Larry Gelbart and Simon Muntner
Directed by: Larry Gelbart

SOME 38th PARALLELS
Frank tries to distinguish himself by selling the camp garbage, but it's Hawkeye who finds a use for it: he dumps it on a troublesome colonel.
Guest Cast: William Christopher, George O'Hanlon, Jr., Lynette Mettey, Richard Lee Sung, Kellye Nakahara, Ray Poss.
Written by: John Regier and Gary Markowitz
Directed by: Burt Metcalfe

DER TAG
Potter decides Frank would be less of a pain if the others were more friendly to him; they oblige, with some startling results.
Guest Cast: William Christopher, Joe Morton, John Voldstad, George Simmons, Kellye Nakahara, William Grant.
Written by: Everett Greenbaum and Jim Fritzell
Directed by: Gene Reynolds

THE NOVOCAINE MUTINY
Frank has Hawkeye up on charges of mutiny for various infractions when Potter was away on leave and Frank was the C.O.
Guest Cast: William Christopher, Ned Wilson, Johnny Haymer, Patricia Stevens.
Written by: Burt Prelutsky
Directed by: Harry Morgan

THE MORE I SEE YOU
Hawkeye is reunited with a woman he thought was out of his life forever, but who never altogether leaves.
Guest Cast: William Christopher, Blythe Danner, Mary Jo Catlett.
Written by: Larry Gelbart and Gene Reynolds
Directed by: Gene Reynolds

THE INTERVIEW
A stateside television correspondent interviews M*A*S*H personnel.
Guest Cast: William Christopher, Clete Roberts.
Written by: Larry Gelbart
Directed by: Larry Gelbart

---

* FIFTH SEASON 1976–1977 *

Regular Cast: Alan Alda, Gary Burghoff, Larry Linville, Mike Farrell, Harry Morgan, Loretta Swit, Jamie Farr, William Christopher.

Executive Producer: Gene Reynolds. Produced by Don Reo, Alan Katz, and Burt Metcalfe.

BUG OUT (1 Hour Show)
After a rumor grows out of proportion, the 4077th moves out, assured that the Chinese are about to attack. Hawkeye, B.J. and Hot Lips remain behind as they are in the middle of critical surgery. All is well when Chinese are pushed back and the camp returns.
Guest Cast: Richard Lee Sung, Frances Fong, Don Eitner, Barry Cahill; Peter Zapp, James Lough, Eileen Saki, Ko-Ko Tani.
Written by: Jim Fritzell and Everett Greenbaum
Directed by: Gene Reynolds

MARGARET'S ENGAGEMENT
Margaret, calling from Tokyo, holds the camp in suspense until she returns with the news of her engagement to Lieutenant Colonel Donald Penobscott. Frank Burns takes the news hard and arrests a Korean family as spies.
Written by: Gary Markowitz
Directed by: Alan Alda

HAWK'S NIGHTMARE
After Hawkeye bemoans the young age of the wounded, he appears to develop problems. Sleepwalking and bad dreams, according to Dr. Sidney Freedman, are taking Hawkeye back to a simple time, but the horrors of war continue to intrude. After assurance by Dr. Freedman that he is as sane as can be, Hawkeye's life once again seems to settle down.
Guest Cast: Allan Arbus, Patricia Stevens, Sean Roche.
Written by: Burt Prelutsky
Directed by: Burt Metcalfe

LT. RADAR O'REILLY
After an offer of promotion made by Master Sergeant Woodruff at a poker game, Radar is promoted to the rank

Burt Metcalfe *(center)* and cast.

of lieutenant. Finding this position awkward, Radar opts to return to his position as an enlisted man.
Guest Cast: Sandy Kenyon, Johnny Haymer, Pat Stevens, Jeff Maxwell, Raymond Chao.
Written by: Everett Greenbaum and Jim Fritzell
Directed by: Alan Rafkin

OUT OF SIGHT, OUT OF MIND
While fixing a stove that explodes, Hawkeye's face is badly burned. His eyes are bandaged, and it is not known if he will ever see again. Meanwhile Frank bets on the outcome of a baseball game which he has already heard. After much tension in the camp the bandages come off, and happily, Hawkeye can see again.
Guest Cast: Tom Sullivan, Judy Farrell, Enid Kent, Dudley Knight, Bobbie Mitchell, Michael Cedar, Kellye Nakahara.
Written by: Ken Levine and David Isaacs
Directed by: Gene Reynolds

THE GENERAL'S PRACTITIONER
In the midst of Hawkeye's being considered, much to his distaste, as a general's personal physician, Radar becomes a surrogate father to a GI Korean baby and wife.
Guest Cast: Edward T. Binns, Leonard Stone, Suesie Elene, Larry Wilcox, Barbara James.
Written by: Burt Prelutsky
Directed by: Alan Rafkin

THE ABDUCTION OF MARGARET HOULIHAN
After hearing that North Korean prisoners have been released in the area, everyone is upset when Margaret disappears. Colonel Flagg is called in and bungles things in his usual manner. Finally Hot Lips returns, after helping in the birth of a Korean baby.
Guest Cast: Edward Winter, June Kim, Le Quynh, Susan Bredhoff, Lynne Marie Stewart, Susan Sakimoto.
Written by: Allan Katz and Don Reo
Story by: Gene Reynolds
Directed by: Gene Reynolds

THE NURSES
When Hot Lips confines Nurse Baker to her quarters, little does she know that Baker's husband has arrived in the camp. Hawkeye and B.J. put them together in Hot Lips' tent, telling everyone that a quarantined patient has been placed there. When Hot Lips discovers what has happened, she breaks down and refuses to press charges.
Guest Cast: Linda Kelsey, Mary Jo Catlett, Carol Lawson Locatell, Patricia Sturges, Gregory Harrison, Jo Ann Thompson.
Written by: Linda Bloodworth
Directed by: Joan Darling

DEAR SIGMUND
Major Sidney Freedman, feeling depressed, visits the 4077th to observe how they fare under the pressures of war. He begins a letter to Sigmund Freud as a form of

self-therapy. Freedman releases his tension in the form of a practical joke with B.J., aimed at Frank Burns.
Guest Cast: Allan Arbus, Charles Frank, Bart Braverman, Sal Viscuso, J. Andrew Kenny, Jennifer Davis.
Written by: Alan Alda
Directed by: Alan Alda

THE COLONEL'S HORSE
While Colonel Potter goes to Tokyo on R & R, his horse develops colic, Klinger becomes chronically depressed, and Hot Lips gets appendicitis. The horse is flushed out with a hose, Hawkeye and B.J. perform an appendectomy on Hot Lips, and all are well when Potter returns, except Klinger. Potter offers Klinger a discharge for severe depression, and Klinger gets very excited, which loses him the discharge.
Guest Cast: Kellye Nakahara.
Written by: Jim Fritzell and Everett Greenbaum
Directed by: Burt Metcalfe

MULCAHY'S WAR
After Frank discovers that Danny Fitzsimons has shot himself to get out of combat, Father Mulcahy is called in. Realizing his lack of understanding of the fighting, Mulcahy accompanies Radar to an aid station where they encounter the fighting. Mulcahy performs an emergency tracheotomy guided by Hawkeye on the radio.
Guest Cast: Ric Mancini, Brian Byers, Richard Foronjy, Wm. Berton Snider, Jeff Maxwell, Ray Poss.
Written by: Richard Cogan
Directed by: George Tyne

HAWKEYE GET YOUR GUN
After 24 hours of surgery, Hawkeye and Potter venture off to a Korean hospital to lend a hand. Hawkeye is appalled to learn that he must carry a gun. After helping the Koreans, they are shelled on the way back. They scramble from the jeep before it is shelled, and Potter urges Hawkeye to shoot in self-defense, against Hawkeye's will.
Guest Cast: Mako, Richard Doyle, Jae Woo Lee, Thomas Botosan, Jeff Maxwell, Phyllis Katz, Carmine Scelza.
Written by: Jay Folb
Story by: Gene Reynolds and Jay Folb
Directed by: William Jurgensen

THE KOREAN SURGEON
When Syn Paik, a North Korean surgeon, arrives with some wounded, he is passed off as a South Korean by Hawkeye and B.J., but to no avail. Hot Lips and Frank try to convince Potter that Paik is a spy. Paik, Hawkeye and B.J. agree that it would be in the interest of all for Syn to leave.
Guest Cast: Soon-Tech Oh, Robert Ito, Larry Hama, Richard Russell Ramos, Dennis Troy.
Written by: Bill Idelson
Directed by: Gene Reynolds

EXORCISM
After Potter orders Radar to move a Korean spirit post believed to ward off evil spirits, things mysteriously begin to go wrong. When an old Korean man is brought into camp for medical attention, he refuses surgery unless the end spirits in the camp are exorcised. A priestess is brought in who exhibits her dance and her bells and chants. All is well, and Radar returns the spirit post to its original position.
Guest Cast: Virginia Ann Lee, James Canning, Philip Ahn, Young Hee Choi, Arthur Song, Jon Yune, Dennis Troy, Barbara James.
Written by: Jay Folb
Story by: Gene Reynolds and Jay Folb
Directed by: Alan Alda

END RUN
Billy Tyler, a young black sergeant, is brought into camp with a bullet wound in the leg. He is a football player, and when he discovers that his leg has been amputated, he wants to die. After talks with Radar, Billy agrees that he must live on.
Guest Cast: Henry Brown, Johnny Haymer.
Written by: John D. Hess
Directed by: Harry Morgan

PING PONG
Lieutenant Colonel Harold Becket lies wounded in post-op waiting to get back to the front for thirty more days of combat duty to get his promotion. Meanwhile, Cho Lin, the Ping Pong champ, is engaged to Soony. He leaves to get her a ring, when he is drafted by the South Korean army. He arrives at the 4077th as a wounded soldier, and after being patched up he is married at the camp.
Guest Cast: Richard Narita, Frank Maxwell, Sachiko Penny Lee, Robert Phalen, Enid Kent, Jeff Maxwell, Roy Goldman, Gil Park.
Written by: Sid Dorfman
Directed by: William Jurgensen

THE MOST UNFORGETTABLE CHARACTERS
Radar gets accepted to the "Famous Las Vegas Writers School" and begins to write his impressions of the camp. It happens to be Frank's birthday, so Hawkeye and B.J. stage a fight with each other to make Frank happy.
Guest Cast: Jeff Maxwell.
Written by: Ken Levine and David Isaacs
Directed by: Burt Metcalfe

SOUVENIRS
Korean children and American soldiers are often badly wounded when they hunt for souvenirs which the enemy has booby-trapped. Potter asks for it to stop, and Hawkeye and B.J. put a local junk dealer out of business.
Guest Cast: Michael Bell, Brian Dennehy, Scott Mulhern, June Kim, Crandal Jue, Alvin Kim.
Written by: Burt Prelutsky
Story by: Burt Prelutsky and Reinhold Weege
Directed by: Joshua Shelley

MARGARET'S MARRIAGE
Prompted by pressure from Frank, Hot Lips sets a date for marriage with Lieutenant Colonel Donald Penobscott. When Donald arrives in camp for the wedding, a bridal shower and bachelor party are given. While he has passed

out drunk, Hawkeye and B.J. place Donald in a body cast and convince him that he has broken his leg. The ceremony is performed and Donald and Hot Lips leave for a week's honeymoon in Tokyo.
Guest Cast: Beeson Carroll, Judy Farrell, Patricia Stevens, Lynne Marie Stewart, Kellye Nakahara, Ray Poss.
Written by: Everett Greenbaum and Jim Fritzell
Directed by: Gene Reynolds

38 ACROSS
Befuddled by a crossword puzzle, Hawkeye persuades Potter to get his old friend Tippy Brooks brought into camp. Tippy is a whiz at puzzles, and amidst many casualties, he provides the needed solution to the puzzle.
Guest Cast: Dick O'Neill, Oliver Clark.
Written by: Jim Fritzell and Everett Greenbaum
Directed by: Burt Metcalfe

HANKY PANKY
Nurse Carrie Donovan receives a "Dear Jane" letter from her husband and practically falls apart. B.J. consoles her, and they spend the night together. Feelings of guilt come over B.J. until he discusses them with Donovan and the air is cleared.
Guest Cast: Ann Sweeny.
Written by: Gene Reynolds
Directed by: Gene Reynolds

HEPATITIS
Father Mulcahy comes down with infectious hepatitis while B.J. performs a very difficult operation and Hawkeye deals with a psychosomatic back pain.
Guest Cast: Barbara James.
Written by: Alan Alda
Directed by: Alan Alda

MOVIE TONIGHT
As a cure for the increased tension at the 4077th, Potter gets a film and makes a social event out of it. As the film continues to break, tensions rise, until Mulcahy plays the piano, Radar does his impersonations, and everyone acts out scenes from the film.
Guest Cast: Enid Kent, Judy Farrell, Jeffrey Kramer, Carmine Scelza.
Written by: Gene Reynolds, Don Reo, Allan Katz and Jay Folb
Directed by: Burt Metcalfe

POST OP
In the midst of a deluge of patients and their individual medical histories, the 4077th is out of blood. Everyone in camp is donating blood at 48-hour intervals when a truckload of Turkish soldiers arrive to offer their blood and save the day.
Guest Cast: Hilly Hicks, Daniel Zippe, Richard Beauchamp, Alan McRae, Gary Springer, Andrew Bloch, John-Anthony Bailey, Sal Viscuso, Andy Romano, Zitto Kazann.
Written by: Ken Levine and David Isaacs
Story by: Gene Reynolds and Jay Folb
Directed by: Gene Reynolds

* SIXTH SEASON 1977–1978 *

Regular Cast: Alan Alda, Gary Burghoff, David Ogden Stiers, Mike Farrell, Harry Morgan, Loretta Swit, Jamie Farr, William Christopher.

All sixth season shows produced by Burt Metcalfe.

FADE OUT, FADE IN (1 Hour Show)
After Margaret leaves for her honeymoon, Frank becomes very distraught, so Potter sends him on R & R. All throughout a deluge of casualties, the 4077th receives reports of a Frank Burns gone berserk. Potter calls Tokyo and requests a replacement surgeon. Major Charles Emerson Winchester III is assigned to the 4077th. Frank Burns is apprehended, promoted, and transferred to a VA hospital in Indiana. Winchester is made a permanent part of the 4077th staff.
Guest Cast: James Lough, Raymond Singer, Tom Stovall, Rick Hurst, Robert Symonds, William Flatley, Kimiko Hiroshige, Joseph Burns, Barbara James, Ray Poss, and Robert Holmes Pettee, Jr.
Written by: Jim Fritzell and Everett Greenbaum
Directed by: Hy Averback

LAST LAUGH
Madness strikes as B.J. and his old friend Bardonaro play a series of practical jokes on each other as Bardonaro is about to leave Korea.
Guest Cast: James Cromwell, Robert Karnes, John Ashton, Duane Tucker, Jo Ann Thompson.
Written by: Everett Greenbaum and Jim Fritzell
Directed by: Don Weis

FALLEN IDOL
At Hawkeye's suggestion, Radar goes to Seoul to find a woman at the Pink Pagoda. He never gets there because of shelling along the way. He is flown into the 4077th, where Hawkeye, feeling tremendous guilt, performs an operation to save Radar. They have a falling out as they lose respect for each other's actions. All is well in the end as Hawkeye pins a Purple Heart on Radar after he has recuperated.
Guest Cast: Frances Fong, Patricia Stevens, Robin Riker, Larry Gilman, Michael Talbott, Roy Goldman.
Written by: Alan Alda
Directed by: Alan Alda

With guest star Edward Winter as Colonel Flagg.

IMAGES
Radar notices a number of tattoos on one of the wounded and convinces himself that with a tattoo he will be irresistible to women. Everyone tries to discourage him, and he admits to having received a tattoo that will wash off.
Guest Cast: Susan Blanchard, Larry Block, John Durren, Judy Farrell, Enid Kent, Rebecca Taylor, Carmine Scelza, Joseph Hardin.
Written by: Burt Prelutsky
Directed by: Burt Metcalfe

WAR OF NERVES
The 4077th, caught up in tension and nerves, creates a bonfire to release their pressure. Meanwhile Sidney Freedman is depressed by a soldier who blames him for his injuries because Freedman had sent him back into combat.
Guest Cast: Allan Arbus, Johnny Haymer, Michael O'Keefe, Peter Riegert, Robert Hilton.
Written by: Alan Alda.
Directed by: Alan Alda

THE WINCHESTER TAPES
Hawkeye tries unsuccessfully to get to Seoul to see a Nurse Gilmore for the weekend. Meanwhile, Winchester has taped a letter home asking for his influential parents to help get him back to the States. To get even, Hawkeye and B.J. switch Winchester's clothes, causing Winchester to alter his eating patterns.
Guest Cast: Thomas Carter, Kimiko Hiroshige.
Written by: Everett Greenbaum and Jim Fritzell
Directed by: Burt Metcalfe

THE LIGHT THAT FAILED
With supplies low, the 4077th gets a truckload of ice cream churns and salt tablets. B.J. receives a mystery novel that everyone in camp reads in turn. The last page is missing and the solution to the mystery is never discovered.
Guest Cast: Gary Erwin, Garret Pearson, Philip Baker Hall, Enid Kent.
Written by: Burt Prelutsky
Directed by: Charles S. Dubin

TEA AND EMPATHY
With British and American casualties heavy, the 4077th's supply of penicillin has been stolen. Father Mulcahy discovers the location of some penicillin, and he and Klinger go out in search of it. They are shot at, but safely return with the drug and save the day.
Guest Cast: Chris Winfield, Chris Mulkey, Neil Thompson, Hap Lawrence, Kerry Mahan, Neil Hunt, James Booth, Sal Viscuso, Gwen Farrell, Barbara James,

Barnetta McCarthy.
Written by: Bill Idelson
Directed by: Don Weis

THE GRIM REAPER
Colonel Victor Bloodworth predicts that 280 wounded will arrive at the 4077th. Hawkeye is antagonized by Bloodworth and shoves him against a wall. Bloodworth presses for a court martial until he becomes one of the wounded and watches Hawkeye saving a soldier's life. Realizing Hawkeye's value as a doctor, Bloodworth drops all charges.
Guest Cast: Charles Aidman, Jerry Houser, David Lyman, Kellye Nakahara.
Written by: Burt Prelutsky
Directed by: George Tyne

THE M*A*S*H OLYMPICS
Realizing how out of shape the 4077th is, Potter decides to hold a camp Olympic competition. The winning team get a three-day pass, so everyone is excited. Donald Penobscott arrives and is allowed to substitute for an ailing Klinger. Hawkeye's team wins, and B.J. must then chauffeur Hawkeye around in a wheelchair for a week.
Guest Cast: Mike Henry, Michael McManus, Michael Payne, Chuck Hicks.
Written by: Ken Levine and David Isaacs
Directed by: Don Weis

IN LOVE AND WAR
Hawkeye falls in love with Kyong Soon, a Korean woman who is caring for her sick mother and orphaned children. All hope is lost as Kyong takes her possessions and the children to the south after her mother has died.
Guest Cast: Kieu Chinh, Alvin Kim, Susan Krebs, Soorah Ahn, Enid Kent, Donald S. Kim.
Written by: Alan Alda
Directed by: Alan Alda

CHANGE DAY
Charles plots a scheme to get rich when he discovers that blue scrip is going to be exchanged for red scrip. Hawkeye and B.J. outsmart him, and he is left holding the worthless scrip.
Guest Cast: Phillip Ahn, Noel Toy, Glenn Ash, Richard Lee Sung, Thomas Dever, Peter Riegert, Johnny Haymer.
Written by: Laurence Marks
Directed by: Don Weis

PATENT 4077
In need of a special surgical clamp, Hawkeye and B.J. hire Mr. Shin, a local jewelry dealer, to make the clamp. Days later the clamp is used to save the leg of a wounded soldier.
Guest Cast: Pat Stevens, Brenda Thomson, Harry Gold, Johnny Haymer, Keye Luke.
Written by: Ken Levine and David Isaacs
Directed by: Harry Morgan

THE SMELL OF MUSIC
Charles plays a French horn and drives Hawkeye and B.J. crazy. They refuse to bathe until the French horn playing is stopped. Meanwhile Potter saves the life of a suicidal patient. The camp collectively hoses down Hawkeye and B.J. while Margaret runs over the French horn with a jeep.
Guest Cast: Richard Lee Sung, Nancy Steen, Lois Foraker, Jordan Clarke, Kellye Nakahara, Barbara James.
Written by: Jim Fritzell and Everett Greenbaum
Directed by: Stuart Miller

COMRADE IN ARMS (Two Parts)
While en route to the 8063rd to demonstrate an arterial transplant operation, Hawkeye and Hot Lips are caught in military fire and are forced to take cover when their jeep stalls. They spend the night in each other's arms.
Guest Cast: Jon Yune, James Saito.
Written by: Alan Alda
Directed by: 1st Part—Burt Metcalfe; 2nd Part—Alan Alda

THE MERCHANT OF KOREA
After Charles hands B.J. two hundred dollars, he begins to take advantage. Everyone gets together and persuades Charles to play poker. He has incredible beginner's luck until Radar discovers that Charles whistles loudly when he bluffs. They all win back their money and then some.
Guest Cast: Johnny Haymer.
Written by: Ken Levine and David Isaacs
Directed by: William Jurgensen

WHAT'S UP DOC?
Hot Lips, believing herself to be pregnant, asks Hawkeye to test her. The only rabbit available is Radar's pet Fluffy. Hawkeye promises not to kill the rabbit while performing the test. Meanwhile, Greenleigh, a patient, holds Charles and B.J. at gunpoint, demanding to be sent back to Ohio. Greenleigh collapses from loss of blood, and Hot Lips isn't pregnant.
Guest Cast: Charles Frank, Lois Foraker, Phyllis Katz, Kurt Andon.
Written by: Larry Balmagia
Directed by: George Tyne

POTTER'S RETIREMENT
Potter is upset when General Kent informs him that people in the 4077th are complaining about his leadership. Potter returns to camp and discovers that the complaints are coming from a Corporal Joe Benson sent by a disturbed Colonel Frank Webster who has been wounded some months earlier.
Guest Cast: Johnny Haymer, George Wyner, Peter Hobbs, Ken White, Enid Kent.
Written by: Laurence Marks
Directed by: William Jurgensen

MAIL CALL THREE
After a delay of three weeks, five sacks of mail arrive, and everyone in camp reacts to good and bad news from

home. Hawkeye receives love letters addressed to Benjamin Pierce, B.J.'s wife has been approached by another man, and Radar's mom has found a boyfriend.
Guest Cast: Oliver Clark, Jack Grapes, Carmine Scelza, Terri Paul.
Written by: Everett Greenbaum and Jim Fritzell
Directed by: Charles S. Dubin

DR. WINCHESTER AND MR. HYDE
Charles takes amphetamines to keep up his energy level, and even drugs Radar's mouse so that it will win a race against a Marine's mouse.
Guest Cast: Chris Murney, Joe Tornatore, Ron Max, Rod Gist.
Written by: Ken Levine, David Isaacs and Ronny Graham.
Directed by: Charles S. Dubin

MAJOR TOPPER
With the possibility of contaminated morphine, the doctors at the 4077th administer placebos to the patients which seem to work. Meanwhile a new soldier is released on a Section 8.
Guest Cast: Andrew Bloch, Donald Blackwell, Hamilton Camp, Peter Zapp, Paul Linke, John Kirby, Michael Mann, Kellye Nakahara.
Written by: Allyn Freeman
Directed by: Charles S. Dubin

YOUR HIT PARADE
With the arrival of a shipment of records, Radar plays the part of a disc jockey and helps to get everyone through the incredibly long deluge of wounded.
Guest Cast: Ronny Graham, Johnny Haymer, Ken Michelman, William Kux, Patricia Stevens, Dennis Troy.
Written by: Ronny Graham
Directed by: George Tyne

TEMPORARY DUTY
With a temporary transfer of personnel between the 4077th and the 8063rd, Hawkeye is replaced by Captain Roy Dupree. Fearing this to be permanent, Charles and B.J. successfully conspire to have Dupree permanently removed from the 4077th.
Guest Cast: George Lindsey, Enid Kent, Marcia Rodd.
Written by: Larry Balmagia
Directed by: Burt Metcalfe

* SEVENTH SEASON 1978–1979 *

Regular Cast: Alan Alda, Gary Burghoff, David Ogden Stiers, Mike Farrell, Harry Morgan, Loretta Swit, Jamie Farr, William Christopher.

All seventh season shows produced by Burt Metcalfe.

PEACE ON US
Hawkeye becomes so disgusted with the stalled Panmunjon peace talks that he impulsively takes matters into his own hands and goes to the meetings to lend a hand.
Guest Cast: Kevin Hagen, Hugh Gillan.
Written by: Ken Levine and David Isaacs
Directed by: George Tyne

B.J. PAPA SAN
B.J. becomes almost the surrogate father to a Korean family. Finding them a substitute for his own absent family, B.J. spends so much time with them that his medical efficiency begins to suffer, and Hawkeye worries about his health.
Guest Cast: Dick O'Neill, Mariel Aragon, Chao-Li-Chi, Johnny Haymer, Stephen Keep, Richard Furukawa, Shizuko Hoshi.
Written by: Larry Balmagia
Directed by: James Sheldon

BABY, IT'S COLD OUTSIDE
While everyone is complaining about the record cold snap, Charles becomes the most unpopular man in camp when his parents send him a winterized polar suit that he insists on flaunting in front of the freezing medical personnel.
Guest Cast: Terry Wills, Teck Murdock, David Dramer, Jan Jordan.
Written by: Gary David Goldberg
Directed by: George Tyne

COMMANDER PIERCE
Hawkeye undergoes a drastic change when he becomes temporary commander of the 4077th and learns about the tedious bureaucracy and accompanying headaches that Colonel Potter deals with daily.
Guest Cast: James Lough, Andrew Massett, Jan Jorden, Enid Kent, Kellye Nakahara.
Written by: Ronny Graham
Directed by: Burt Metcalfe

THE BILLFOLD SYNDROME
Charles becomes so irate over a turndown for a future medical position at home that he refuses to talk to anyone in the unit, and a young soldier can't remember his own identity.
Guest Cast: Kevin Geer, Alan Arbus.
Written by: Ken Levine and David Isaacs
Directed by: Alan Alda

LIL
Colonel Potter strikes up a warm friendship with the visiting Eighth Army head nurse, Colonel Lil Rayburn, a

Klinger jokes with Radar and Hot Lips during a scene in the officers' club.

regular Army type of his own age and interests. But Radar reacts huffily, thinking his commanding officer has more than just friendship on his mind.
Guest Cast: Carmen Mathews, Perrin Page.
Written by: Sheldon Bull
Directed by: Burt Metcalfe

THEY CALL THE WIND KOREA
A strong windstorm affects the M*A*S*H personnel in varying ways: Hawkeye and most of the unit busy themselves securing items that could blow away, Radar prepares his animal hutch for the worst, while a disgusted Charles switches his Tokyo-leave transportation from air to ground and runs into a difficult medical situation en route to Seoul.
Guest Cast: Enid Kent, Tom Dever, Paul Cavonis, Randy Stumpf.
Written by: Ken Levine and David Isaacs
Directed by: Charles S. Dubin

OUR FINEST HOUR (1 Hour Show; Black & White)
Newscaster Clete Roberts, reprising an earlier interview appearance, returns to update Korean War conditions when he conducts a series of television talks with the leading characters of the 4077th.
Guest Cast: Clete Roberts.
Written by: Ken Levine and David Isaacs, Larry Balmagia, and Ronny Graham
Directed by: Burt Metcalfe

NONE LIKE IT HOT
The oppressive Korean heat gets to everyone, especially Klinger, who responds to the conditions with an ingenious scheme to effect a discharge. Meanwhile, Hawkeye and B.J. are secretly gloating over their newly arrived remedy for the weather until they realize that if word gets out it could spoil their fun.
Guest Cast: Johnny Haymer, Ted Gehring, Jan Jorden, Kellye Nakahara, Jeff Maxwell.
Written by: Ken Levine, David Isaacs, and Johnny Bonaduce
Directed by: Tony Mordente

OUT OF GAS
Heavy casualties are arriving, creating severe problems for the M*A*S*H unit because they are nearly out of pentothal. Mulcahy takes up a collection from everyone—including a case of wine from Charles' private supply—and he and Charles take the jeep to make a trade with the black marketeers for pentothal.
Written by: Tom Reeder
Directed by: Mel Damski

MAJOR EGO
Charles assumes heroic proportions after reviving a dying patient with heart massage, and he becomes more insufferable than ever when a photojournalist from *Stars and Stripes* arrives to publicize his medical prowess.
Guest Cast: Greg Mullavey, David Dean, Frank Pettinger,

Phyllis Katz, Patricia Stevens.
Written by: Larry Balmagia
Directed by: Alan Alda

DEAR COMRADE

Hawkeye and B.J. discover that Charles is living the life of Riley thanks to the attentions of his menially paid Korean servant, a man of unusual skills. He has an important contribution to make—a native remedy for a seemingly insoluble medical problem.

Guest Cast: Sab Shimono, Larry Block, Todd Davis, David Dozer, Dennis Troy, Wayne Long, Robert Clotworthy, James Saito.
Written by: Tom Reeder
Directed by: Charles S. Dubin

AN EYE FOR A TOOTH

Father Mulcahy takes being passed over for promotion philosophically until he hears of the rapid advancement made by a heroic helicopter pilot. Then his uncharacteristically bold actions stun Colonel Potter and the entire company.

Guest Cast: Peter Palmer, Russell Takaki.
Written by: Ronny Graham
Directed by: Charles S. Dubin

POINT OF VIEW

In this unique episode, the camera becomes the eyes of a young wounded soldier. It records his sensory responses to being wounded, flown by helicopter to the 4077th, examined, operated on, and treated in post-operation.

Guest Cast: Brad Gorman, Marc Baxley, Edward Gallardo, Jan Jorden, Hank Ross, David Stafford, Paul Tuerpe.
Written by: Ken Levine and David Isaacs
Directed by: Charles S. Dubin

PREVENTIVE MEDICINE

The number of arriving wounded has increased because of a careless Colonel Lacy. Hawkeye slips Lacy something to make him ill and removes his appendix under the strong protests of B.J.

Guest Cast: James Wainwright, Larry "Flash" Jenkins.
Written by: Tom Reeder
Directed by: Tony Mordente

DEAR SIS

Father Mulcahy writes a pre-Christmas letter home to his sister, who is a nun. His frustration at not being more effective at the 4077th seems to represent the general depression of the unit's personnel as they approach the holiday season thousands of miles away from their loved ones.

Guest Cast: Lawrason Driscoll, Patrick Driscoll, Jo Ann Thompson, Jeff Maxwell, W. Perren Page.
Written by: Alan Alda
Directed by: Alan Alda

THE PRICE

The 4077th is confronted by two crises: Colonel Potter's mare, Sophie, mysteriously disappears from her corral, and Hawkeye and B.J. find themselves with a young Korean boy on their hands who is trying to avoid conscription into the Army.

Guest Cast: Miko Mayama, Yuki Shimoda, Ken Mochizuki, Jeff Maxwell, Johnny Haymer, Dennis Sakamoto.
Written by: Erik Tarloff
Directed by: Charles S. Dubin

HOT LIPS IS BACK IN TOWN

Radar, who is smitten with the cute new nurse at the hospital, relies on Hawkeye's expertise on how to cope with the situation. Hot Lips, meanwhile, celebrates her just-granted divorce by taking a step that arouses Colonel Potter's ire.

Guest Cast: Petty Lee Brannan, Walter Brooke, Jan Jorden, Enid Kent, Kellye Nakahara.
Written by: Larry Balmagia and Bernard Dilbert
Directed by: Charles S. Dubin

INGA

It's instant attraction for Hawkeye when a beautiful Swedish doctor arrives to observe combat surgery. That is, until she upstages him in the operating room with a superior technique and his ego is bruised.

Guest Cast: Mariette Hartley.
Written by: Alan Alda
Directed by: Alan Alda

THE YOUNG AND RESTLESS

A lecture on the latest techniques by a young surgeon from Tokyo and a later demonstration of his surgical skill bring home to the resident M*A*S*H surgeons that they are out of touch with new medical practices.

Guest Cast: Peggy Lee Brennan.
Written by: Mitch Markowitz
Directed by: William Jurgensen

AIN'T LOVE GRAND

The impossible happens for the snobbish Charles when he shares an emotional experience with Klinger, who discovers a U.S. nurse who finds him and his bizarre attire attractive, while Charles succumbs to the exotic charms of a Korean girl he meets at the bar.

Guest Cast: Kit McDonough, Sylvia Chang, Eileen Saki, Michael Williams, Judy Farrell.
Written by: Ken Levine and David Isaacs
Directed by: Mike Farrell

C•A•V•E

The 4077th evacuation to a nearby cave to avoid U.S. artillery fire on a Chinese target poses another hazard for Hawkeye, who has a claustrophobia problem that Colonel Potter is unaware of.

Guest Cast: Basil Hoffman, Enid Kent, Mark Taylor, Charles Jenkins.
Written by: Larry Balmagia and Ronny Graham
Directed by: William Jurgensen

THE PARTY

Talk of a post-war reunion suggests an idea to B.J.: plan-

ning a present-day stateside gathering of 4077th families, a scheme he continues to promote even under the duress of "bugging out" in the wake of a Chinese breakthrough.
Written by: Burt Metcalfe and Alan Alda
Directed by: Burt Metcalfe

RALLY ROUND THE FLAGG, BOYS
The sinister Colonel Flagg pops up at the 4077th again, playing his usual spy games, convinced that Hawkeye is a communist sympathizer.
Guest Cast: Ed Winter, Neil Thompson, Bob Okazaki, Jerry Fujikawa, James Lough.
Written by: Mitch Markowitz
Directed by: Harry Morgan

A NIGHT AT ROSIE'S
Hawkeye, B.J., and their medical cohorts find a new way to escape the depressing atmosphere of the war, much to the displeasure of Colonel Potter.
Guest Cast: Keye Luke, Joshua Bryant, Joseph de Reda, Eileen Saki, Richard Lee Sung.
Written by: Ken Levine and David Isaacs
Directed by: Burt Metcalfe

DREAMS
The 4077th can't escape the Korean War, even in its dreams. Exhausted after two days without sleep, members of the 4077th steal away for cat naps and experience dreams that reveal their fears, yearnings and frustrations.
Guest Cast: Ford Rainey, Rick Waln, Robin Haynes, Catherine Bergstrom, Fred Stuthman, Kurtis Sanders, Ray Lynch, Kellye Nakahara, Connie Izay, Dennis Troy.
Written by: Alan Alda
Story by: Alan Alda and James Jay Rubinfier
Directed by: Alan Alda

* EIGHTH SEASON 1979–1980 *

Regular Cast: Alan Alda, David Ogden Stiers, Mike Farrell, Harry Morgan, Loretta Swit, Jamie Farr, William Christopher.
All eighth season shows produced by John Rappaport and Jim Mulligan. Executive producer Burt Metcalfe.

TOO MANY COOKS
A clumsy foot soldier finds the quickest way to the crew's heart, boosting morale at the war-weary 4077th by cooking gourmet delights. Only Colonel Potter, burdened with a personal crisis, is immune from the high spirits enveloping the hospital.
Guest Cast: Gary Burghoff, John Randolph, Ed Begley, Jr.
Written by: Dennis Koenig
Directed by: Charles S. Dubin

ARE YOU NOW, MARGARET?
A Congressional aide visits the 4077th on a supposedly routine fact-finding tour, but it's discovered that his motives are far deeper.
Guest Cast: Lawrence Pressman, Jennifer Davis, Jeff Maxwell.
Written by: Thad Mumford and Dan Wilcox
Directed by: Charles S. Dubin

GUERILLA MY DREAMS
The arrival of a wounded Korean woman sparks a conflict at the 4077th: Hawkeye wants to heal her, but a steely ROK officer is more anxious to "question" her about alleged guerilla activities.
Guest Cast: Mako, Joshua Bryant, Haunani Minn, George Kee Cheung, Marcus Mukai, Connie Izay.
Written by: Bob Colleary
Directed by: Alan Alda

PERIOD OF ADJUSTMENT
Klinger, taking over as the 4077th's new clerk, wearies of complaints about his inefficiency, while B.J.'s homesickness is intensified by news of Radar's visit to his family.
Guest Cast: Jeff Maxwell, Eileen Saki, Jan Jorden, Gwen Farrell.
Written by: Jim Mulligan and John Rappaport
Directed by: Charles S. Dubin

PRIVATE FINANCE
A South Korean woman misinterprets Klinger's motives when he tries to aid her daughter financially. Meanwhile, Hawkeye wrestles with his conscience over a promise made to a dying soldier.
Guest Cast: Shizuko Hoshi, Denice Kumagai, Mark Kologi, Joey Pento, Philip Simma, Art Evans.
Written by: Dennis Koenig
Directed by: Charles S. Dubin

MR. AND MRS. WHO?
Charles Winchester returns to the 4077th after a trip to Tokyo with an uncharacteristic hangover and the uneasy feeling of a romantic entanglement. Meanwhile, the hospital struggles to find a cure for an outbreak of deadly hemorrhagic fever.
Guest Cast: Claudette Nevins, James Keane.
Written by: Ronny Graham
Directed by: Burt Metcalfe

THE YALU BRICK ROAD
Hawkeye and B.J. lose their way while rushing urgently needed antibiotics to the 4077th, which is wracked with food poisoning. Wandering back to M*A*S*H , the pair are found by a peculiar North Korean soldier.

Guest Cast: Soon-Teck Oh, G. W. Bailey, Bob Okazaki, Kimiko Hiroshige, Roy Goldman, Kellye Nakahara, Jeff Maxwell, Byron Chung.
Written by: Mike Farrell
Directed by: Charles S. Dubin

NURSE DOCTOR
A beautiful and ambitious young nurse who plans to become a doctor when she leaves the Army finds herself in a misunderstanding with Father Mulcahy. Meanwhile, the camp's water supply is depleted, and the rest of the 4077th is more concerned about where to find a running shower.
Guest Cast: Alexandra Stoddart, Jeff Maxwell, Kellye Nakahara.
Written by: Sy Rosen, Thad Mumford and Dan Wilcox
Story by: Sy Rosen
Directed by: Charles S. Dubin

LIFE TIME
A severely wounded soldier, rushed to the poorly equipped 4077th by chopper, will die or be permanently paralyzed if he doesn't receive major surgery in 20 minutes. Nearly all of the action in this innovative episode is compressed into the program's 25-minute running time.
Guest Cast: Kevin Brophy, William Berton Snider, J.J. Johnston, Kellye Nakahara, Roy Goldman, Joann Thompson, Jeff Maxwell.
Written by: Alan Alda and Walter D. Dishell, M.D.
Directed by: Alan Alda

GOODBYE RADAR (Part One)
Company clerk Radar O'Reilly (Gary Burghoff), on leave in Tokyo, is desperately needed back at the crisis-stricken 4077th, but his return is delayed by outside events. While casualties continue to pour in from the front, the 4077th's generator conks out, depriving the medical unit of all electrical power. But Klinger, filling in for the vacationing Radar, lacks the expertise and experience to wheel and deal for a new machine.
Guest Cast: Gary Burghoff, Marilyn Jones, Johnny Haymer, Michael O'Dwyer, Richard Lee-Sung, Tony Cristino, Arell Blanton.
Written by: Ken Levine and David Isaacs
Directed by: Charles S. Dubin

GOODBYE RADAR (Part Two)
As company clerk Radar O'Reilly reluctantly prepares to depart the 4077th, the unit is still without electricity due to a broken generator, and the operating room continues to fill up with war wounded as night falls. The responsibility for procuring a new generator falls on Klinger, who lacks Radar's masterful knack of cutting through red tape in search of much-needed supplies.
Guest Cast: Gary Burghoff, Lee De Broux, Whitney Rydbeck, David Dozer, W. Perren Page, Jon St. Elwood, Gwen Farrell, David Heveran.
Written by: Ken Levine and David Isaacs
Directed by: Charles S. Dubin

DEAR UNCLE ABDUL
Klinger discovers that his duties as company clerk include catering to the eccentric whims of the 4077th officers. Consequently, the unusual demands by Klinger's superiors leave little time to write a letter home to Toledo.
Guest Cast: Kelly Ward, Richard Lineback, Alexander Petals, Bob Hill.
Written by: John Rappaport and Jim Mulligan
Directed by: William Jurgensen

CAPTAINS OUTRAGEOUS
A brawl at Rosie's Bar puts Rosie in the hospital, and the 4077th doctors are pressed into service as temporary saloonkeepers. Meanwhile, Father Mulcahy is apprehensive that his long-pending promotion to captain will again be denied.
Guest Cast: Eileen Saki, John Orchard, Sirri Murad, G. W. Bailey, Paul Cavonis, Momo Yashima, Joann Thompson.
Written by: Thad Mumford and Dan Wilcox
Directed by: Burt Metcalfe

STARS AND STRIPE
Friction arises between B.J. and Winchester when they're asked to write a report for a prestigious medical journal on how they saved a soldier's life with a daring operation. Meanwhile, Hot Lips receives an eventful visit from Scully, her combat soldier beau.
Guest Cast: Joshua Bryant, Jeff Maxwell.
Written by: Dennis Koenig
Directed by: Harry Morgan

HEAL THYSELF
Colonel Potter turns crotchety when he catches the mumps, and his condition is worsened when another M*A*S*H member gets the same disease and has to move in with him. A temporary replacement surgeon is quickly brought into the 4077th and seems to be a gem in terms of both personality and ability.
Guest Cast: Edward Herrmann, Jennifer Davis, Gwen Farrell.
Written by: Dennis Koenig
Story by: Dennis Koenig and Gene Reynolds
Directed by: Mike Farrell

YESSIR, THAT'S OUR BABY
A baby born to a Korean woman and an American GI is abandoned at the 4077th. Knowing that mixed-blood children are often mistreated in Korean society, the troop sets about the frustrating task of finding a new home for the infant.
Guest Cast: William Bogert, Howard Platt, Yuki Shimoda, Elizabeth Farley, Christopher Tankersley.
Written by: Jim Mulligan
Directed by: Alan Alda

BOTTLE FATIGUE
Horrified by the gigantic size of his monthly bar tab at the officers' club, Hawkeye vows to give up booze for a week. Meanwhile, Winchester desperately tries to halt his sis-

ter's impending marriage to a man he considers unworthy of the Winchester heritage.
Guest Cast: Shelly Long, Jeff Maxwell, David Hirokane, Shari Saba.
Written by: Thad Mumford and Dan Wilcox
Directed by: Burt Metcalfe

MORALE VICTORY
Tired of their constant complaints about the quality of recreational activities at the 4077th, Colonel Potter appoints Hawkeye and B.J. as the new morale officers. Winchester's morale has already reached a new peak. He's ecstatic about his operation on a wounded soldier which saved the boy's leg, leaving only "negligible" side effects.
Guest Cast: James Stephens, G. W. Bailey, Jeff Maxwell, Connie Izay.
Written by: John Rappaport
Directed by: Charles S. Dubin

OLD SOLDIERS
Hawkeye is appointed temporary commander of the 4077th when Colonel Potter rushes off to Tokyo on a mysterious mission. While in command, Hawkeye's main problem is housing a large group of Korean refugees comprised mainly of rambunctious children who need medical care.
Guest Cast: Jane Connell, Sally Imamura, Jason Autajay.
Written by: Dennis Koenig
Directed by: Charles S. Dubin

LEND A HAND
Irritated that the 4077th is planning a "surprise" party for him, Hawkeye volunteers to go to the aid of a wounded surgeon at the front. An additional irritant to Hawkeye is the arrival of Dr. Borelli, a wisecracking medical adviser with whom he habitually disagrees.
Guest Cast: Robert Alda, Antony Alda, Daren Kelly, Shari Saba.
Written by: Alan Alda
Directed by: Alan Alda

GOODBYE, CRUEL WORLD
Klinger redecorates his quarters, but the resultant ridicule he receives drives him to new heights in his efforts to get out of the Army. Meanwhile, the doctors are perplexed by the reaction of an Asian-American war hero when he's informed that he's being sent home because of his wounds.
Guest Cast: Clyde Kusatsu, Allan Arbus, Philip Burns, Kellye Nakahara, James Lough, David Cramer.
Written by: Thad Mumford and Dan Wilcox
Directed by: Charles S. Dubin

APRIL FOOLS
A no-nonsense Colonel who is notorious as a hard-nosed disciplinarian visits the 4077th during an outbreak of April Fools' Day pranksterism. Colonel Potter tries in vain to halt the mayhem before Colonel Daniel Webster Tucker arrives in camp.
Guest Cast: Pat Hingle, G. W. Bailey, Roy Goldman, Jennifer Davis.
Written by: Dennis Koenig
Directed by: Charles S. Dubin

WAR CO-RESPONDENT
B.J. finds himself attracted to a famous war correspondent who has fallen in love with him.
Guest Cast: Susan Saint James, Brad Wilkin, Calvin Levels.
Written by: Mike Farrell
Directed by: Mike Farrell

BACK PAY
Angered by the way civilian doctors stateside are profiting from the war, Hawkeye presents the Army with a bill for his medical services. Meanwhile, Charles reluctantly demonstrates American medical practices to three Korean medics.
Guest Cast: Sab Shimono, Peter Kim, Jerry Fujikawa, G. W. Bailey, Richard Herd, Roy Goldman.
Written by: Thad Mumford, Dan Wilcox and Dennis Koenig
Directed by: Burt Metcalfe

And Now A Word From The Viewers

Some Fan Mail

Illustrating the impact M*A*S*H has around the world, a fan living in Toledo wrote Jamie Farr the following:

*You might be interested to know that at The Medical College of Ohio, in Toledo, where I work as a lab technician, we recently had a symposium for the world's top anatomists and physiologists from forty countries. Several of the doctors from South American countries who have seen M*A*S*H there wanted to "eat at that place Corporal Klinger talks about." So they were taken to Tony Packo's for dinner!*

After the 1979 Emmys were telecast, QUBE, the "interactive" cable system of Columbus, Ohio sent Loretta Swit a mailgram:

We don't care what the Academy says. The people of Columbus, Ohio, think your work is the best. The QUBE audience chose you as their favorite. On behalf of the QUBE viewers, we'd like to say thanks for your fine work in the past, and we wish you continued good luck in the future.

After viewing the episode "Old Soldiers," a viewer wrote to Harry Morgan:

*Every Monday night, I am home to watch M*A*S*H. To my family, 9:00 is my time. Even Monday night football gets second priority for at least half an hour. Whoever does the casting must have a sixth sense. Usually, when a person is replaced on a good show, it goes down the drain as far as I'm concerned, but not M*A*S*H. First B.J., excellent; then Charles, superb; and then my Colonel Potter, of which words escape me. That part was written for you, and you know it. It fits you like a glove or vice versa. Every week I laugh, I cry, and I feel all the angers and frustrations that you all feel with your characters. It's very hard to imagine there isn't a 4077th. Tonight you tore my heart out and put it back in upside-down. I sobbed. Your toast to your departed friends was an Emmy in itself. If they don't give you one, I'll have one made up personally and keep it at my house for you.*

A young fan taken with the character of Colonel Potter wrote to Harry Morgan:

*I am a 14-year-old M*A*S*H fanatic. I never miss it. I think you're wonderful as Potter. I like Potter much better than Henry Blake, even though I cried when he died. When Potter first came to the show, I thought he was going to be a dud. But you're a great actor, and you turned Potter into a sensitive person.*

A viewer, impressed with the talent and skill of Harry Morgan, wrote to him:

Colonel Potter is the culmination and the showcase of a gentleman who truly knows his profession. If all professional people—doctors, politicians, lawyers, engineers, and others—were as outstanding and knowledgeable at what they do as you, this would be a fine world to live in.

After watching the "Old Soldiers" episode another viewer, obviously taken with Harry Morgan's skill and talent, wrote:

I have always believed that the craft of acting depends on energy and believability. A good performance in theater, of any kind, will bring the audience into the scene and involve him—make him more than just a dispassionate spectator, more than just a casual observer. This is part of the magic of acting. Last night you gave me—and millions of others, I think—a lesson in what magic is really all about. I will count your performance as one of the most moving experiences I have ever witnessed on television or live stage. It would be easy enough to credit the writers and the director and to say that the actors are only chess pieces. Perhaps this is so in certain schools of acting, and we have all seen performers move as just pieces, without feeling and without understanding. But for even a dramatic reading to really reach its audience, we depend on the person to convey the sense and to bring, from whatever experiences or motivation he chooses, life to the part he is portraying. In honoring us with your performance last night in particular, and through your whole association with the series, you have brought honor to your profession. I most sincerely hope it has given you as much satisfaction as it has given us joy and compassion. Thank you for your gift.

The Swamp (on Stage 9)

A letter to David Ogden Stiers reads:
The character of Frank Burns seemed a weak contrast to Hawkeye and B.J., but Charles Emerson Winchester seems to be much more of an equal match! I'm not sure whether I love or hate him. However ostentatious he may be, though, anyone who loves classical music shouldn't be considered a total loss.

Commenting about the production, another viewer wrote:
One question does come to mind and, although I don't wish to criticize, I am curious. All of you have an obvious respect for the material and for one another; nevertheless, why can't that respect extend to the audience? Specifically, why in heaven's name does such a fine program resort to canned laughter? It really is an unnecessary adornment. The opinion of my friends and I (albeit an uneducated one) is that it adds nothing and sometimes proves bothersome or even insulting.

A young viewer wrote to Jamie Farr:
*M*A*S*H is my favorite TV show. Everytime my mom and dad see you on M*A*S*H, they crack up. My dad says you look like my Aunt Mary when he sees you wearing a short dress or skirt, because you have hairy arms and legs just like her. Ha, ha. It's true.*

An enthusiast who had visited the set of M*A*S*H later wrote:
*When visiting M*A*S*H, I was struck by the congenial atmosphere among the cast. To see such fine people create something of such quality in such a positive atmosphere fills me with a powerful sense of optimism.*

A mother writes to Loretta Swit:
I asked my son what he would like for his birthday. His answer was, "Loretta Swit." This remark led into one of the best conversations we have had in quite some time. He tells me that you are what he would consider the ideal women, e.g. a nice smile, pleasing voice, nice hair, and that you come across on television as having a terrific sense of humor. When I added that you were also Polish, his answer was, "That helps."

A male fan writes Loretta Swit:
*It's bad enough that you and your zany cohorts on M*A*S*H have me in stitches at least once a week, but when I sit down to dinner and ask my wife, "What's this?" to have her answer, "Loretta Swit's porkchops"—well, as Jack Benny would say,*

Alan with his brother Antony Alda and father Robert Alda.

*it isn't exactly cricket, Miss Swit. At 58 years of age, my tummy is already well developed (to say the least), and considering M*A*S*H gives me a few dozen belly laughs each week, the bigger my belly, the bigger the pain! Yes, indeed, your porkchops were delicious and I'll thank you to keep your ruddy recipes to yourself in the future—or at least tell me how you can eat such food without making a pig of yourself and losing your yummy figure.*

Reacting to the change in cast from Trapper John to B.J. Hunnicut, a viewer wrote Mike Farrell:

B.J. turned out to be more than an adequate replacement. In fact, the whole beauty of the B.J. character is that he is not a replacement at all. He is very much a new individual at the 4077th and, by the time he arrived at the camp (drunk out of his mind) on that first episode, I was too intrigued with B.J.'s potential to do more than wish Trapper a safe flight home.

After a M*A*S*H symposium at the University of California, Los Angeles, the cast received the following letter:

*Yesterday resounded with the continuous laughter and applause of a group of people having an immensely enjoyable time. The wonder of M*A*S*H is that, through the laughs, we are gaining powerful insights about the pain and passion of human endeavors. You and fellow members of your ensemble proved to the privileged 400 in our enthusiastic audience at "A Day in the Life of M*A*S*H" how you accomplish that feat week after week. The intelligence, respect, and sensitivity which color the way you work with one another must be the key to your success.*

A very touching letter to Mike Farrell declares:

*I am a M*A*S*H nut. You are a super actor. (I must admit that when Wayne Rogers left the show, I was a little nervous, but after one episode, I knew all was well.) You and Alan Alda have the ability to make me laugh and cry during the same half hour (and you make me not ashamed of crying, which, at age 17, is a bad thing to do). I just want you to know how much M*A*S*H means to me, not only as a comedy, but as a point to stop and think about my life. I know it's only television, but is it? Allow me to confide in you, sir. I once used drugs, not much, but more than enough. Indirectly, and yet directly, you are why I'm no longer using drugs. You are why I got myself together before it was too late. I now make A's and B's in high school and hope to study medicine in college. Thank you, Mr. Farrell, for straightening me out. (Thank Alan for me, too!)*

Another touching observation comes from a fan who writes to Mike Farrell:

I just saw the show in which B.J. goes into a drunk after reading of Radar's visit with his family. What a service you did for men, by having the courage and sensitivity to portray B.J.'s emotions and vulnerabilities so openly.

A letter to Alan Alda analyzes the emotion his performance stirs in one viewer:

I feel it is a gift of love you are sharing and yet, I, as the recipient, am in a very frustrating position. Your gift of love stirs almost every emotion we have—warmth, compassion, love, hate, anger, fear, ego, and mistrust. It is extremely difficult to have these emotions stirred and not be able to turn around and exchange or share my own love, yet I cannot honestly say I love you because I don't know you. I guess the most honest thing I can say is that you appear to be a person of admirable qualities and talents, and I wanted to share that with you. I feel many people have one or the other, but few have both. I've received a great deal from you through your talents, and I wish to thank you for the love you have sent.

A thoughtful letter is written by another caring fan:

*M*A*S*H seems to have invented a category of entertainment all its own. Truly human would best describe M*A*S*H for me. I guess what I'm trying to say is that, as a teacher, especially a religious teacher, I wouldn't mind my kids imitating the compassion and dedication of a Hawkeye Pierce, the fidelity of a B.J. Hunnicut, the seemingly stoic, yet caring, heart of a Margaret Houlihan, or the innocent gentleness of a Radar O'Reilly. I also wouldn't mind if my students were inspired to have peace and not war, justice and not hatred, and to strive to ease pain and not cause it.*

A viewer comments:

*The beauty is that M*A*S*H doesn't have to show string bikinis, murder, rape, sex, violence, and other various vulgarities to obtain good, solid ratings.*

From yet another correspondent:

*M*A*S*H is not the funniest show on television but merely because it does not choose to be. It makes statements and makes them believable without the preaching that mars so many other programs that try to be "socially significant."*

*M*A*S*H seems to be the only comedy show that can successfully combine its message with fine entertainment. M*A*S*H proves that art and television are not mutually exclusive.*

From another letter:

*The development, the depth, the individuality of each character began to grow—and became people living with hell and horror. The comedy was still there, of course, but underneath—the strength and compassion and anger at human destruction began to show. Something wonderful was happening for me. I was no longer watching excellent actors working closely in a good series. I was watching people I cared about and was proud to know—as multidimensional as my closest friends. I get angry when Hawkeye turns chauvinistic because of Inga, then sit and grin because my friend Hawkeye reverted to his real self. I hurt with Radar when his idol crumbles and cry when he and his very human friend smile at each other in regained friendship. I understand Hawkeye's walking on furniture to release tension. I filled a wastebasket with soggy tissues when Margaret's parents went to B.J.'s reunion together because they loved her enough to put aside personal differences. The wastebasket overflowed when Radar read his letter. So many episodes, some touching me deeply, some making me laugh, some bringing back memories of worrying about friends serving in Korea. Even though I know M*A*S*H must end some season, I'll cry then, too, because I will miss my friends very much.*

Another viewer comments:

*I've been a M*A*S*H fan for years, and I'm always amazed at how much humor, compassion, anger, and pathos can be packed into the space of a few minutes with such satisfying results. Another reason I am drawn to the show is what it reveals about myself. There are times when I feel that I have lost the ability to respond emotionally to people and their situations, but when I watch M*A*S*H, I discover that often I am moved to tears, that I am still able to cry. I thank you—the cast, the writers, and crew—for reminding me that I am still human.*

From the letter of another fan:

*I practically risk life and a limb barreling up the highway every night to catch the first M*A*S*H program of the evening, at 5:30. I fly in the front door, turn on the set, then take off my coat. That leaves me an hour and a half to feed the cats, do the laundry, make supper, and wash dishes before the second M*A*S*H of the evening at 7:30. Then, I can relax until the third one of the evening at 11:30. I guess I'm what you might call a fan.*

An exhausted Hawkeye catches 40 winks.

A viewer writes of the show's effect on patients in a nursing home:

*I am a registered nurse, and I've seen what happiness M*A*S*H has brought to patients. In fact, in the nursing home I work at now, we have to be sure we wake a patient from his nap in time for the show every day.*

A letter written to Jamie Farr becomes almost poetic:

*I'm a 15-year-old boy who, by no fault of his own, fell deeply in love with old movies and the golden age of television. Because of this I have come to believe that there is a dearth of excellence on modern television. But there are exceptions to this and, by gosh, M*A*S*H is one heck of an exception. M*A*S*H is like running barefoot on an open field of grass in the summer; it's like a cool swim in a clear lake on a hot afternoon; it's like your first kiss; it's like standing up on water skis for the first time and feeling the rush of wind on your chest; like going down a snow-covered hill on a sled. M*A*S*H is all the good things of life, even though it is set in the most fallacious place in the world. M*A*S*H is a classic.*

A minister was so taken with the show that he wrote to say:

*This is unabashedly a fan letter. More than that, it is also an admission of extreme personal jealousy. Your sermons are often more eloquent and compassion filled than are mine. It is also an attempt to tell you just how much I appreciate this long-running morality play that you choose to call M*A*S*H. I must also tell you that I have difficulty with M*A*S*H, for just when I think that I have you safely tucked into bed in that ambiguous thing called comedy, you come along with something like last evening's program, jarring me completely out of my comfortable frame of reference, leaving me shaking in my boots (no pun intended). I was in high school during the Korean War years, and, though I heard often that war is hell, somehow I swallowed the glamorous, adventure come-on promised by the recruiting posters and believed that war was a kind of gentleman's sport that was necessary. It was not until the Vietnam years that I actually internalized the truth about war. Oh, I read the statistics which told us that so many died or had been wounded, so many bridges destroyed, and so much of the enemy's supply destroyed, but very few of those statistics ever dealt with the awesome construction of the human mind. Those who believe that war is necessary and unavoidable should be required to sit through at least 1,000 screenings of last night's program [an episode called "The Billfold Syndrome"] before declaring it necessary. Possibly, combined gatherings of their leaders, as well as ours, should see it together. The coping mechanisms that these people use are absolutely amazing, especially the two levels of withdrawal from reality that were portrayed by David Ogden Stiers and Kevin Geer, the last of which prompts this letter. The scenes depicted Sergeant Neilson's withdrawal and B.J., Hawkeye, and Major Freedman's attempt to reach him. What came through to me was the extraordinary compassion of the three and the deep need of that one. My prayer is that those who saw this will see that it is all right for men to cry. There is nothing wrong with hugging and being hugged. There is nothing inherently dirty in needing to be understood and to be touched in a caring way. Part of my own work is to help fathers understand that it is perfectly proper for a father to hug his son and for them to express their love for each other. Your writers, and Mr. Arbus, and Mr. Geer preached a more eloquent sermon than I will be able ever to preach. Let me thank you again for the many evenings that you have helped to fill with laughter and, just as surely, thank you for those which you have helped to fill with tears."*

Alan discusses sound considerations with sound man Steve Bass.

In response to the death of Henry Blake, hundreds of letters were received. This one is typical of many:

The episode where Henry Blake was discharged was great—marvelously done, with humor and tenderness and, even, perhaps, a tear or two. Although we don't see how the show can be as good without him—since he was leaving—this was a beautiful way of easing him out. But why in hell kill him off? It doesn't advance the story any, and it turns the series we have looked to for warmth and laughs into a tragedy, leaving a bad taste in the mouth. In general, I felt like my daughter—we were both spluttering over it the rest of the evening—when she said, "It was just dumb, dumb, dumb!" So, I'm sure you can do something about it. There could have been a mistake—perhaps the plane wasn't really the one he took, or he missed it because of—whatever—a traffic jam, or a pressing engagement—or anything, in Tokyo—or even perhaps there were survivors, picked up by a fishing trawl, or whatever. Anything, so long as our funny, warm guy gets home to his wife and kids. I know in war not everyone did get home, but not everyone didn't, either—and I feel that this was a senseless killing. Mistakes are often made in wartime about such things. Let's rectify this one. We never have to see Henry again, but let's keep the memories sweet and happy and funny, not clouded with sorrow."

Another example of the responses to the death of Henry Blake came from a viewer who wrote:

I think I understand the message the writers were trying to convey. My question is: Was it necessary? Was it necessary to put all of us through the agony and pain of losing someone we had come to know well, and yes even to love, to the senselessness of war? Through the usual excellent writing and fine acting, I was able to feel Henry's joy at finally escaping the chaotic nightmare his humor had helped to make bearable for the others. Particularly in these times when there is adversity on so many fronts, was it necessary to rekindle the pain and feelings of helplessness and frustration that all caring Americans feel about the seemingly endless dying? I never thought I'd be opting for escapism, but now I feel as though I am carrying another sadness—another loss. Please believe me, we know—we care—we pray to see the killing end; but please leave us our entertainment!

From another prespective, a viewer writes:

The show in which McLean Stevenson was written out was one of the finest examples of superb writing, directing, and acting I have ever seen on television. I had heard that two endings had been filmed. I was pleased to see that the possibly "more touchy" version was shown. I have the greatest respect for the individuals involved in that final decision.

A teenager writes:

*The actors seem as if they are as gentle and caring of others on the set as they are off of it. I am discovering more and more often in my life that love is the key that can keep people, families, and nations together. Even our small bickerings can be the basis of war. It's very important to have such a show as M*A*S*H on TV. Maybe this show can, in some way, instill in us another way of living.*

Extolling the qualities of M*A*S*H another viewer says:

*M*A*S*H represents what the true capacity of television should be—to educate and to entertain! I respect every creative person on your show—from producer to grip. I thank God you all decided at one point in your lives to pursue your talents so that television can be, for at least one half hour a week, a real pleasure to watch.*

A very perceptive viewer writes:

First of all, I would like to take this opportunity to express my deep appreciation for all the time and energy that it takes to produce excellent shows week after week. I suppose that most of the mail is directed to the stars, and the producers are left out in the cold. And yet, without you there wouldn't be any show to watch. Unfortunately, most people take the finished product for granted and don't think at all about the problems you have to deal with while filming. . . . Even though your contributions are not as "visible" as those of the cast, they are nevertheless as important and I thank you for all your efforts. . . . The only flaw that I see in the series is the treatment of women. For a series that is very liberal in all other aspects, it still remains rather sexist. I find it disturbing that the audience knows the first names of all the male characters, but that all the other women, besides Margaret, are known as Nurse Able, Baker, or Kelly. I'm sure they have first names, too. Frankly, I would like to get to know the nurses a lot better, and it would be a refreshing change every once in a while to see the show through their eyes.

In response to the episode "Point of View" a fan says:

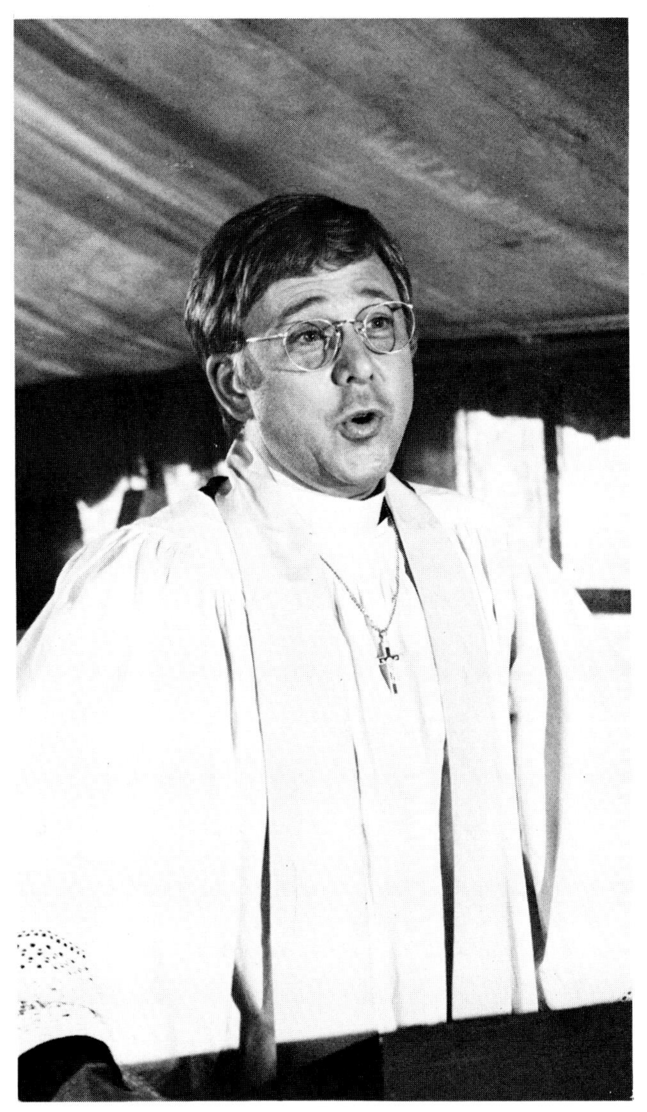

Leading a religious service.

*Thank you. Your latest episode, showing us a soldier with throat wounds and a view of M*A*S*H through his own eyes, is the best episode I've seen. It combined an interesting technique with the usual superior writing and directing. Through the eyes of that soldier you revealed to the audience the warmth and caring that your great TV series is all about.*

Another viewer responds to the same episode:

The depths of the characters have never come across so clearly before as they did tonight. The patient's view of the company was a real way to bring out the basic kindness of those who have been scrapping with one another in so many episodes.

One fan writes:

*M*A*S*H is an incredible show of sheer genius, fantastically well written and equally well acted. The humor is exquisitely touching—so intensely human! A perfect balance of every emotion. I hope M*A*S*H will stay on forever.*

A registered nurse says, in response to the episode "Point of View":

Your show last night had tremendous insight. I especially liked the way Hawkeye presented himself and explained to the patient what he was going to do at every moment. In my experience as a nurse, I have found that explanation proves to be so very important. What you showed takes so little time, but is so very valuable to a patient in a crisis situation. Honesty is another thing I admired about the show and the point of not making doctors and nurses into God—like figures who know all—but into real people, humans who don't know all, but can instill a confidence in a patient that is, in itself, invaluable.

Another viewer expresses a deeply serious response to the show:

*I have never wanted a series to end more. An end to the M*A*S*H series would mean an end to that war, and if every viewer LIVES each of your shows as I do, I'm sure they would agree. You have conveyed a very deep message to millions; a message that not only applied to the Korean war but also to the Vietnam war and every war, battle, or skirmish that preceded it. God forbid we have to go through those kinds of hell again. Thank you for what you have given the world, and for God's sake keep carrying the message—and maybe some day those responsible for wars will open their eyes.*

And from one of the younger viewers of M*A*S*H comes this heartfelt letter:

Dear Alen
How are you?
Im fine.
I saw one of the episodes that you dreamed every time you close your eyes some old man took one of your arms and you went down the river in the boat and saw a kid got shot in the belly.
Would you please explain to me thank you.
Can I have a picture of the hole cast. sign it pleace thank you.
Im interested in acting can I have your advice in what college to go and your personal advice about it.
In your character as a doctor talking to B.J. some times I go to the dictionary to find what the words mean.

*The Winner—M*A*S*H*

Chronology of Awards and Nominations

*DENOTES WINNERS

1973

Academy of Television Arts and Sciences—Emmy Awards

OUTSTANDING COMEDY SERIES—Gene Reynolds, Producer
OUTSTANDING NEW SERIES—Gene Reynolds, Producer
OUTSTANDING CONTINUED PERFORMANCE BY AN ACTOR IN A LEADING ROLE IN A COMEDY SERIES—Alan Alda
OUTSTANDING PERFORMANCE BY AN ACTOR IN A SUPPORTING ROLE IN COMEDY—Gary Burghoff
OUTSTANDING PERFORMANCE BY AN ACTOR IN A SUPPORTING ROLE IN COMEDY—McLean Stevenson
OUTSTANDING DIRECTORIAL ACHIEVEMENT IN COMEDY—Gene Reynolds, M*A*S*H Pilot
OUTSTANDING WRITING ACHIEVEMENT IN COMEDY—Larry Gelbart, M*A*S*H Pilot
OUTSTANDING ACHIEVEMENT IN FILM EDITING FOR ENTERTAINMENT PROGRAMMING—Stanford Tischler and Fred W. Berger

Hollywood Foreign Press Association—Golden Globe Awards

BEST COMEDY SHOW—M*A*S*H
BEST ACTOR IN A COMEDY OR MUSICAL—Alan Alda

Directors' Guild Awards

* GENE REYNOLDS—M*A*S*H Pilot

Writers' Guild Awards

* Teleplay by LARRY GELBART, "Chief Surgeon Who?"

American Cinema Editors—Eddie Awards

* FRED W. BERGER, A.C.E.—"Bananas Crackers & Nuts"
STANFORD TISCHLER, A.C.E.—M*A*S*H Pilot

1974

Academy of Television Arts and Sciences—Emmy Awards

* OUTSTANDING COMEDY SERIES—Gene Reynolds and Larry Gelbart, Producers
* BEST LEAD ACTOR IN A COMEDY SERIES—Alan Alda
* ACTOR OF THE YEAR—SERIES—Alan Alda
BEST SUPPORTING ACTOR IN COMEDY—Gary Burghoff
BEST SUPPORTING ACTOR IN COMEDY—McLean Stevenson
BEST SUPPORTING ACTRESS IN COMEDY—Loretta Swit
* BEST DIRECTING IN COMEDY—Jackie Cooper, "Carry On, Hawkeye"
BEST DIRECTING IN COMEDY—Gene Reynolds, "Deal Me Out"
BEST WRITING IN COMEDY—Linda Bloodworth and Mary Kay Place, "Hot Lips and Empty Arms"
BEST WRITING IN COMEDY—McLean Stevenson, "The Trial of Henry Blake"
BEST FILM EDITING FOR ENTERTAINMENT PROGRAMMING—Stanford Tischler and Fred W. Berger

Hollywood Foreign Press Association—Golden Globe Awards

BEST ACTOR IN A COMEDY OR MUSICAL—Alan Alda
BEST SUPPORTING ACTRESS IN A TELEVISION SHOW—Loretta Swit

Alan at the People's Choice Awards.

Directors' Guild Awards

GENE REYNOLDS—"Deal Me Out"

Writers' Guild Awards

Teleplay by BERNARD DELBERT, LARRY GELBART and LAURENCE MARKS;
Story by BERNARD DELBERT, "Carry On Hawkeye"
Teleplay by LARRY GELBART and LAURENCE MARKS, "The Incubator"
Teleplay by LAURENCE MARKS;
Story by SHELDON KELLER, "Radar's Report"
Teleplay by CARL KLEINSCHMITT, "Sometimes You Hear The Bullet"
Teleplay by BRUCE SHELLY and DAVID KETCHUM, "Tuttle"

American Cinema Editors—Eddie Awards

* FRED W. BERGER, A.C.E. and STANFORD TISCHLER, A.C.E., "The Trial of Henry Blake"

1975

Academy of Television Arts and Sciences—Emmy Awards

OUTSTANDING COMEDY SERIES—Gene Reynolds and Larry Gelbart, Producers
OUTSTANDING LEAD ACTOR IN A COMEDY SERIES—Alan Alda
OUTSTANDING CONTINUING PERFORMANCE BY A SUPPORTING ACTOR IN A COMEDY SERIES—Gary Burghoff
OUTSTANDING CONTINUING PERFORMANCE BY A SUPPORTING ACTOR IN A COMEDY SERIES—McLean Stevenson
OUTSTANDING SINGLE PERFORMANCE BY A SUPPORTING ACTOR IN A COMEDY OR DRAMA SERIES—Harry Morgan, "The General Flipped At Dawn"
OUTSTANDING CONTINUING PERFORMANCE BY A SUPPORTING ACTRESS IN A COMEDY SERIES—Loretta Swit
* OUTSTANDING DIRECTING IN A COMEDY SERIES—Gene Reynolds, "O.R."
OUTSTANDING DIRECTING IN A COMEDY SERIES—Hy Averback, "Alcoholics Unanimous"
OUTSTANDING DIRECTING IN A COMEDY SERIES—Alan Alda, "Bulletin Board"
OUTSTANDING ACHIEVEMENT IN CINEMATOGRAPHY FOR ENTERTAINMENT PROGRAMMING FOR A SERIES—William Jurgensen, "Bombed"
OUTSTANDING FILM EDITING FOR ENTERTAINMENT PROGRAMMING FOR A SERIES—Stanford Tischler and Fred W. Berger, "The General Flipped At Dawn"

People's Choice Awards

* FAVORITE MALE TELEVISION PERFORMER—Alan Alda (Tie with Telly Savalas)

Hollywood Foreign Press Association—Golden Globe Awards

* BEST ACTOR IN A COMEDY OR MUSICAL—Alan Alda

Directors' Guild Awards

HY AVERBACK, "Alcoholics Unanimous"

Writers' Guild Awards

* Teleplay by LARRY GELBART and LAURENCE MARKS, "O.R."
Teleplay by SID DORFMAN, "Private Charles Lamb"

American Cinema Editors—Eddie Awards

* FRED W. BERGER, A.C.E. and STANFORD TISCHLER, A.C.E., "A Full Rich Day"

1976

Academy of Television Arts and Sciences—Emmy Awards

OUTSTANDING COMEDY SERIES—Gene Reynolds and Larry Gelbart
OUTSTANDING LEAD ACTOR IN A COMEDY SERIES—Alan Alda
OUTSTANDING CONTINUING PERFORMANCE BY A SUPPORTING ACTOR IN A COMEDY SERIES—Gary Burghoff
OUTSTANDING CONTINUING PERFORMANCE BY A SUPPORTING ACTOR IN A COMEDY SERIES—Harry Morgan
OUTSTANDING CONTINUING PERFORMANCE BY A SUPPORTING ACTRESS IN A COMEDY SERIES—Loretta Swit
* OUTSTANDING DIRECTING IN A COMEDY SERIES—Gene Reynolds, "Welcome to Korea"
OUTSTANDING DIRECTING IN A COMEDY SERIES—Alan Alda, "The Kids"
OUTSTANDING WRITING IN A COMEDY SERIES—Larry Gelbart and Gene Reynolds, "Hawkeye"
OUTSTANDING WRITING IN A COMEDY SERIES—Larry Gelbart and Simon Muntner, "Hawkeye"
OUTSTANDING ACHIEVEMENT IN CINEMATOGRAPHY FOR ENTERTAINMENT PROGRAMMING FOR A SERIES—William Jurgensen, "Hawkeye"
* OUTSTANDING FILM EDITING FOR ENTERTAINMENT PROGRAMMING FOR A SERIES—Stanford Tischler and Fred W. Berger, "Welcome To Korea"

People's Choice Awards

FAVORITE TELEVISION COMEDY PROGRAM—M*A*S*H
FAVORITE MALE TELEVISION PERFORMER—Alan Alda

Hollywood Foreign Press Association—Golden Globe Awards

* BEST ACTOR IN A COMEDY OR MUSICAL—Alan Alda

Directors' Guild Awards

HY AVERBACK, "Bombed"

Writers' Guild Awards

Teleplay by LAURENCE MARKS, "Big Mac"
* Teleplay by EVERETT GREENBAUM and JIM FRITZELL and LARRY GELBART, "Welcome To Korea"

American Cinema Editors—Eddie Awards

FRED W. BERGER, A.C.E. and STANFORD TISCHLER, A.C.E.—"Welcome To Korea"

The George Foster Peabody Awards

* FOR BROADCAST EXCELLENCE—M*A*S*H

1977

Academy of Television Arts and Sciences—Emmy Awards

OUTSTANDING COMEDY SERIES—Gene Reynolds, Executive Producer; Allan Katz, Don Reo, and Burt Metcalfe, Producers
OUTSTANDING LEAD ACTOR IN A COMEDY SERIES—Alan Alda
* OUTSTANDING CONTINUING PERFORMANCE BY A SUPPORTING ACTOR IN A COMEDY SERIES—Gary Burghoff
OUTSTANDING CONTINUING PERFORMANCE BY A SUPPORTING ACTOR IN A COMEDY SERIES—Harry Morgan
OUTSTANDING CONTINUING PERFORMANCE BY A SUPPORTING ACTRESS IN A COMEDY SERIES—Loretta Swit
* OUTSTANDING DIRECTING IN A COMEDY SERIES—Alan Alda, "Dear Sigmund"
OUTSTANDING DIRECTING IN A COMEDY SERIES—Joan Darling, "The Nurses"
OUTSTANDING DIRECTING IN A COMEDY SERIES—Alan Rafkin, "Lt. Radar O'Reilly"

People's Choice Award: Mike Farrell, Loretta Swit, Harry Morgan, Alan Alda, William Christopher, Jamie Farr.

OUTSTANDING WRITING IN A COMEDY SERIES—Alan Alda, "Dear Sigmund"
OUTSTANDING CINEMATOGRAPHY IN ENTERTAINMENT PROGRAMMING FOR A SERIES—William Jurgensen, "Dear Sigmund"
OUTSTANDING FILM EDITING IN A COMEDY SERIES—Samuel E. Beetley and Stanford Tischler, "Dear Sigmund"

People's Choice Awards

FAVORITE TELEVISION COMEDY PROGRAM—M*A*S*H
FAVORITE MALE TELEVISION PERFORMER—Alan Alda

Hollywood Foreign Press Association—Golden Globe Awards

BEST TELEVISION SERIES COMEDY OR MUSICAL—M*A*S*H
BEST ACTOR IN A COMEDY OR MUSICAL—Alan Alda

Directors' Guild Awards

* ALAN ALDA, "Dear Sigmund"

Writers' Guild Awards

* Teleplay by ALAN ALDA, "Dear Sigmund"
Teleplay by JAY FOLB;
Story by GENE REYNOLDS and JAY FOLB, "Hawkeye Get Your Gun"

American Cinema Editors—Eddie Awards

STANFORD TISCHLER, A.C.E. and SAMUEL E. BEETLEY, "Dear Sigmund"

Gene Reynolds presents Harry Morgan with the Gold Award of Purple Heart Veterans Rehabilitation Service.

1978

Academy of Television Arts and Sciences—Emmy Awards

OUTSTANDING COMEDY SERIES—Burt Metcalfe, Producer
OUTSTANDING LEAD ACTOR IN A COMEDY SERIES—Alan Alda
OUTSTANDING CONTINUING PERFORMANCE BY A SUPPORTING ACTOR IN A COMEDY SERIES—Gary Burghoff
OUTSTANDING CONTINUING PERFORMANCE BY A SUPPORTING ACTOR IN A COMEDY SERIES—Harry Morgan
OUTSTANDING CONTINUING PERFORMANCE BY A SUPPORTING ACTRESS IN A COMEDY SERIES—Loretta Swit
OUTSTANDING DIRECTING IN A COMEDY SERIES—Burt Metcalfe and Alan Alda, "Comrades In Arms—Part I"
OUTSTANDING WRITING IN A COMEDY SERIES—Alan Alda, "Fallen Idol"
OUTSTANDING FILM EDITING IN A COMEDY SERIES—Stanford Tischler and Larry L. Mills, "Fade Out, Fade In"

People's Choice Awards

* FAVORITE TELEVISION COMEDY PROGRAM—M*A*S*H

* [illegible]ORITE MALE TELEVISION [illegible]RMER—Alan Alda

[illegible]uild Awards

[illegible] and BURT METCALFE, "Comrades [illegible]

[illegible]ild Awards

[illegible]JAMES FRITZELL and EVERETT [illegible]UM, "Fade Out, Fade In"

American Cinema Editors—Eddie Awards

* STANFORD TISCHLER, A.C.E. and LARRY L. MILLS, "Fade Out, Fade In"

1979

Academy of Television Arts and Sciences—Emmy Awards

OUTSTANDING COMEDY SERIES—Burt Metcalfe, Producer

OUTSTANDING LEAD ACTOR IN A COMEDY SERIES—Alan Alda

OUTSTANDING SUPPORTING ACTOR IN A COMEDY OR COMEDY-VARIETY OR MUSIC SERIES—Gary Burghoff

OUTSTANDING SUPPORTING ACTOR IN A COMEDY OR COMEDY-VARIETY OR MUSIC SERIES—Harry Morgan

OUTSTANDING SUPPORTING ACTRESS IN A COMEDY OR COMEDY-VARIETY OR MUSIC SERIES—Loretta Swit

OUTSTANDING DIRECTING IN A COMEDY OR COMEDY-VARIETY OR MUSIC SERIES—Charles S. Dubin, "Point of View"

OUTSTANDING DIRECTING IN A COMEDY OR COMEDY-VARIETY OR MUSIC SERIES—Alan Alda, "Inga"

* OUTSTANDING WRITING IN A COMEDY OR COMEDY-VARIETY OR MUSIC SERIES—Ken Levine and David Isaacs, "Point of View"

OUTSTANDING FILM EDITING FOR A SERIES—Stanford Tischler and Larry L. Mills, "The Billfold Syndrome"

People's Choice Awards

* FAVORITE TELEVISION COMEDY PROGRAM—M*A*S*H

* FAVORITE MALE TELEVISION PERFORMER—Alan Alda

Directors' Guild Awards

CHARLES S. DUBIN, "Point of View"

Writers' Guild Awards

* Teleplay by GARY DAVID GOLDBERG, "Baby It's Cold Outside"

Teleplay by KEN LEVINE and DAVID ISAACS, "Point of View"

American Cinema Editors—Eddie Awards

STANFORD TISCHLER, A.C.E. and LARRY L. MILLS, "The Billfold Syndrome"

1980

People's Choice Awards

* FAVORITE TELEVISION COMEDY PROGRAM—M*A*S*H

* FAVORITE MALE TELEVISION PERFORMER—Alan Alda

* FAVORITE ALL AROUND MALE ENTERTAINER—Alan Alda

Hollywood Foreign Press Association—Golden Globe Awards

* BEST ACTOR IN A COMEDY OR MUSICAL—Alan Alda

Directors' Guild Awards

* CHARLES S. DUBIN, "Period of Adjustment"

Writers' Guild Awards

* Teleplay by THAD MUMFORD and DAN WILCOX, "Are You Now, Margaret?"

Teleplay by JOHN RAPPAPORT and JIM MULLIGAN, "Period of Adjustment"

Teleplay by MITCH MAROWITZ, "The Young and the Restless"

Teleplay by KEN LEVINE and DAVID ISAACS, "Goodbye Rader," Parts I and II

American Cinema Editors—Eddie Awards

* STANFORD TISCHLER, A.C.E. and LARRY L. MILLS, A.C.E., "The Yalu Brick Road"